Morgan Harrington
Murdered and Dead for Good
A Mother's Quest to Find a Serial Killer and Healing

MORGAN HARRINGTON
Murdered
Dead *and* *for* Good

A Mother's Quest to Find a Serial Killer and Healing

GIL HARRINGTON
JANE LILLIAN VANCE

VAJRA BOOKS

Published and Distributed 2017 by
Vajra Books
Jyatha, Thamel, P.O. Box 21779, Kathmandu, Nepal
Tel.: 977-1-4220562, Fax: 977-1-4246536
e-mail: bidur_la@mos.com.np
www.vajrabooks.com.np

ISBN 978-9937-623-77-3

Printed in Nepal

For Morgan, and
the inevitable Next Girl

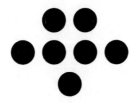

Introduction

—⊶⊷—

Pursuit of the Back to School Killer captured the hearts and minds of millions across America following the murder of my daughter, 20-year-old Virginia Tech coed Morgan Harrington, who vanished on October 17, 2009, during a Metallica concert in Charlottesville, Virginia. Morgan's case created a worldwide firestorm in both traditional and social media, which has never let up. Today, Morgan's name generates 10 million Google hits; she has a Wikipedia page; and police study Morgan's case as the first to harness social media for its crime-solving potential.

Desperate to generate tips that would reveal Morgan's killer, my husband Dan and I participated in hundreds and hundreds of interviews on television, in print, and online. The platforms were both local and national, including *Dr. Phil, Anderson Cooper, Nancy Grace, The Today Show,* and *Good Morning America.* To help find Morgan, Metallica's lead guitarist and vocalist James Hetfield made a heartfelt public service announcement which aired around the world. Several full-length documentaries were filmed: *Disappeared, Voice of America,* and the September 2015 special 2-hour *48 Hours* season premiere, which broke viewing records.

Because of this broad media exposure, Morgan became everyone's daughter. Parents everywhere tuned in, and college students closely followed new developments. True crime fans were riveted. Morgan was missing for an excruciating 100 nights. We directed this tremendous interest and created a foundation, Help Save the Next Girl, to inspire awareness of predatory danger especially around campuses. That message quickly took hold and grew exponentially. Help Save the Next Girl currently shows 65 million Google hits. Chapters are active and spreading in middle schools, high schools, and universities. No wonder: Help Save the Next Girl crackles as this generation's campfire at the crossroads of hot issues, including rape culture, girl shaming, child predators, police accountability, and the correct sentencing for a convicted bone-breaking murderer who kills with his bare hands.

Activism ushered in considerable healing and comfort for our family. Millions were drawn to Morgan's story, seeking tools to manage their own loss and grief. For five years, we worked relentlessly and creatively to find justice for Morgan and to help save the next girl. Shockingly, in September, 2014, the Back to School Killer struck again in Charlottesville. The agonizing abduction and murder of 18-year-old University of Virginia student Hannah Graham finally unmasked Jesse Matthew and led to his arrest and triple trial.

We had done the impossible, found the serial killer hiding in plain sight and stopped him cold, but his capture had come at a terrible price. The Back to School Killer was an apex predator who was implicated in numerous rapes. He pled guilty to the abduction and attempted murder of a 2005 victim, and to abducting and murdering Morgan Harrington and Hannah Graham. He has just begun serving seven consecutive life sentences without the chance of parole in Virginia's notorious, remote Red Onion prison.

The conclusion of Jesse Matthew's prosecution and conviction allows me finally to be more candid and intimate about information in this book than I have previously shared. Included in the narrative are many new anecdotes, and some of Morgan's own unpublished writing and art. Though I realize it may be controversial, I have also included postmortem photographs of our beloved Morgan. Until now, these images have been seen only by family members. I do not intend to shock with these photographs. I believe it is my duty to show the magnitude of loss and devastation we have experienced. What Jesse Matthew did to Morgan is too horrific to convey only with words.

Despite unflinching and direct content, the book is ultimately redemptive, positive, and uplifting. A murdered daughter is an abomination. How can Morgan be Dead for Good? Our insistence on alchemizing evil answers that impossible question.

Morgan Harrington: Murdered and Dead for Good is not a professional detective's crime chronicle. It is a template for response to tragedy, the spontaneous and organic record of the suffering and growth my family experienced following my daughter Morgan's abduction, rape, and murder by the elusive Back to School Killer, Jesse Matthew.

Morgan's death caused an overwhelming tsunami of anguish and pain. Yet almost immediately I began putting my thoughts on paper. Our home was scattered with a confetti of tear-stained post-it notes. Every feeling I captured on paper through a blog, poem, or sketch felt like pulling a shard of glass from a wound. The process hurt, but inevitably promoted healing. In six and a half years, I believe I have journaled myself into some level of insight.

They say it takes a village to raise a child. I know it takes a village to bury one. We have been blessed beyond measure by our community, our friends, and an ever-expanding group of family. We have survived the murder of our daughter because of the outpouring of love, kindness, and compassion we have received. Our family is immensely grateful to each of you.

Always, 241
Gil Harrington
Roanoke, Virginia

Morgan's mother Gil trusted my voice to chronicle the trials of Jesse Matthew. I realized that bringing readers into those charged courtrooms to observe justice unfold would require three skills: my own emotional restraint, precise observation, and an intimate, honest portrait of a mother walking a spiritual tightrope. Gil Harrington not only makes it across the chasms. Her insights during those long-awaited trials rivet and instruct. I believe Gil knows and shows us all a way out of hell.

Jane Lillian Vance
Blacksburg, Virginia

Fracture and Freefall

Part I

Humming to myself, I drove into the garage after church that Sunday. It was 12:30 in the afternoon of October 18, 2009. I was pondering the service and felt lifted and inspired. I walked into our family room and bent to kiss the top of Dan's head. He was settled into his comfy chair and rustling through the Sunday paper like every other week. Then: "Gil, the University of Virginia police called earlier. Morgan's purse was found in the parking lot of the John Paul Jones Arena. Everything is there, though, and the police have her purse in their Lost and Found."

I could almost hear the rumbling as the foundation, the tectonic plates of our life shifted, pulled apart, and split.

Devastation.

I knew immediately in my gut that we were there, at the great divide of our lives, the event that would define our family history into two sections, what took place before, and what took place after this great gaping crevasse opened and obliterated all.

"What do you mean? Where is Morgan? Have you heard from her? If she lost her purse, she would be on that phone either spitting nails or crying. Something terrible has happened to Morgan. Where is she?"

So Dan started calling Morgan's friends.

They were also scared. Morgan had left her seat and her friends, Amy and Sarah, in the arena, to go to the bathroom early in the concert, and she had never returned. Sarah was concerned and called Morgan after twenty minutes. Morgan answered and said she was outside the building, had been repeatedly denied re-entry, and so would find a ride home.

Find a ride home? Morgan's car was in the parking lot.

Sarah said Morgan didn't sound like herself, and Morgan didn't answer any follow-up phone calls. Inside the arena, the crowd kept dancing.

None of this made sense. Crazy, it was crazita. Something was badly wrong.

Morgan had been so excited about attending the Metallica concert at the John Paul Jones Arena at the University Of Virginia in Charlottesville, Virginia. The tickets for the October 17, 2009 concert had been pinned on our refrigerator door, front and center, for months. Morgan wouldn't have walked out and missed the show. How could she find a ride home? Why would she not take her own car in that parking lot near the arena, and why would she leave her friends who had driven with her? She wouldn't.

And her purse--no woman leaves her purse behind. Morgan wouldn't.

Dan called UVA police and reported Morgan as a missing person. "No," he had to emphasize, "It's more than a lost purse. We don't know where our daughter is, and we fear something terrible has happened to her." With that call, the foundations of our reality shifted more, and we entered the purgatory of the missing phase.

October 18, 2009

"Missing" is full blown hell. It is horrific not to know where your precious daughter is. The verbiage doesn't capture in any way the primitive fear a parent experiences with a child missing. I recoil at the word, *missing*, so passive.

Morgan is not missing. My reading glasses are missing, frequently, because I am inattentive and distracted. Morgan has not been misplaced. She has been stolen, robbed, ripped from us.

We are sure that Morgan didn't run away. Anyone would run into Morgan's life.

For twenty years, three months, and two weeks, she had a wonderful life. Our best case scenario was that Morgan was being held against her will.

But how could this be? Where is our girl?

We spend an excruciating, fear-filled night in Morgan's bed, sobbing and sleepless. In the morning, we will travel over Afton Mountain to Charlottesville to meet with University of Virginia police.

October 19, 2009

Dan and I are stunned; feel like zombies as we meet with a room full of law enforcement at the University of Virginia police station. UVA, Charlottesville, Albemarle County, so many police faces and names. Just the sheer number of law enforcement gathered tells us: this ain't good.

John Phillips from Virginia State Police arrives to take primary investigative responsibility. Agent Phillips takes us to Lannigan Field and shows us where Morgan's purse was found. A bloodhound named Grace is brought over to fix on the scent from Morgan's pillowcase.

Helicopters are circling overhead. The intensity of motion and stimulation overwhelms.

Dan and I are frantically trying to process this surreal place in time. Obscene phrases become commonplace in our conversations. Someone instructs: "Bring your daughter's DNA, maybe a hairbrush, or a toothbrush." Someone else: "Do you have Morgan's dental records, or fingerprints?"

Dan and I learned that Morgan had fallen in the arena and was bleeding from a gash on her face. She was crying and disoriented in the arena by the time she reached the bathroom. Somehow, Morgan ended up outside the John Paul Jones arena. She tried repeatedly at two entrances to get back inside to her friends, but was denied re-entry.

Her actions were reported as erratic and bizarre. Morgan was bleeding, and she was sent out into the night.

It was her last night.

On that evening of October 17th, the temperature in Charlottesville hovered around freezing. Morgan's jacket was back inside, with her friends. In one of its pockets was her ticket stub. Several groups of students later reported noticing her, cold, aimless, confused.

My God. Law enforcement are checking the dumpsters for Morgan.

At the end of our meeting, a police officer motions to escort us out of the back entrance to the station, because news media has started to gather in response to the university-wide alert that has been posted about Morgan being missing.

Dan and I look at each other and quickly decide.

No way. We won't just leave and slink away. Who can plead for information about Morgan more sincerely than her parents?

We stand with Virginia State Police in front of the University of Virginia police station. Lieutenant Joe Rader holds the first press conference about a missing student named Morgan Harrington.

Both Dan and I speak, and take questions. We are wooden and stilted, but know our presence, our participation, is correct, our work.

Standing before media, we finally feel something concrete for us to do that may help us find our precious Morgan.

At our core, Dan and I are worker bees, never happier than when we have a job to do. Now we have an action piece, a task to do for Morgan. And we are on it.

Our hospital experience is invaluable in allowing us to compartmentalize our emotions and perform this job, embracing the media as fully as we are able, trying to bring our girl home. Desperate to gain any pertinent information or tip that might help the investigation, we participate unhesitatingly in the dizzying, frantic, growing media storm.

We are inundated with interview requests, both national and local, CBS, NBC, HLN, ABC, WSLS, WDBJ. No time to hide under the covers and cry. We clear the decks and try to engage fully with all media, each request.

One early TV interview with Nancy Grace is harrowing for me. We are miked up, balanced on stools in the studio, waiting for our segment. We are hearing the on-air story in our earpieces, and phrases leap out: I hear "body parts" and the word "dismembered."

I reel on the high stool, ready to throw up, cry, or wet my pants. These moments are surreal, terrible, scary. But there is no place to go, no place to escape from the fact that our daughter is missing.

Of course we give our interview and are coherent. This is what we must do to ride the media storm of interest. At the very worst, at the lowest point of our lives, we must behave the most courageously we ever have. For Morgan.

This schedule of interviews forms the only slender thread of hope we see for Morgan's return. Our kitchen island is cleared of its usual mail, bills, recipes, grocery lists. Everything is pushed aside and a command center is set up for more and more interviews. They continue.

There is a clipboard with interview requests, another clipboard with confirmed interviews, and an infernal confetti of post-its from fractured conversations that may lead somewhere or mean something.

Our son Alex, even from his vantage point of New York City, says our chaos is screaming for infrastructure. We buy a giant white board and markers which we nail to the pantry door. Better order ensues.

The phone is insistent, ringing nonstop. One unexpected and gracious call on day three is from James Hetfield, lead guitarist of Metallica. He asks to speak to Dan.

Mr. Hetfield says, "As fathers, we are outraged that your precious daughter has been stolen. We will help in any way we can to find Morgan."

Metallica is incredibly kind and responsive. Metallica fan club members generate the first Morgan missing poster and disseminate it widely on social media. The band contributes a generous $50,000 towards a reward fund, seeking information in Morgan's case.

Our dear friend Susan Rives arrives with a trunk full of casseroles and her calm wisdom and reassurance. "You are living a messy life right now, but you can do it. I'm here to help." And she does, making it possible for us to participate in dozens of interviews in the next few jet-fueled days. I can't remember to eat. Susan reminds me.

Although it is a really steep learning curve for us, we are supremely motivated to figure out how to present Morgan's story and bring her home. I stagger downstairs in my robe at 5 a.m., letting in one TV crew who begin to set up cameras in the living room. A second crew is there setting up at 9 a.m., in our den. Dan is changing his shirts three and four times a day to give a different look for the cameras on different stations.

Trying to find some way to reach my girl, I write a pleading poem. It's really a desperate letter to Morgan, hiding in a controlled shape. I name the poem *Mogo*, her nickname, a word I want to call my daughter now, beside me, home.

> *MOGO*
> *What a strange place to be*
> *your face staring out from our TV*
> *we carry the numbers of the state police*
> *the phone keeps ringing, there is no peace*
> *guys with cameras traipse through the hall*
> *our life's become a free-for-all*
> *I plead on camera for your release, come home soon Morgan--please.*

Every night, Dan and I fall into bed exhausted, and try to regroup. Our conversation is like something from a war trench, two frightened people whispering in the dark: "Can you do this crazy dance one more day?" "Not sure. It is so hard. I am aching, so sad." "Just commit to one more day. Let's dig deep and do one more day. We can stop tomorrow if you want."

And I say to myself, in the dark, like a pitiful, mumbled, tiny prayer: "I will try not to say *umm* so much, and I will try to look at the camera. Okay? I'll do better tomorrow. And I'll stop saying Morgan *was*. I'll say Morgan *is*; that's our hope. Got it. I will do it. I will do better. I've got to try."

It is a challenging, exhausting process to keep ripping off the bandage and share our loss and despair. But we do.

At this point, there are no case developments to share with media. So instead, we are trying to learn to peel our skins back and let our relationship with Morgan shine through. We are trying to transmit our love for Morgan to the world, hoping it will call her back to our family.

Our pain and our love are the news.

I begin to see. I believe people are called to this story, compelled by the intimacy and intensity of our suffering. They too are searching for tools that may help them navigate the pain of loss when it's their turn. Inevitably, life delivers loss to all of us.

We are surviving so far. We are a test case.

Morgan Dana Harrington was born in 1989, in Charlottesville, Virginia. She was murdered there in 2009. Just 20 years old. Such an unfathomable waste.

Morgan was a beautiful girl, both inside and out. She had a pretty idyllic childhood. Our house was always full of kids, with countless sleepovers, soccer games, piano lessons, forts built in the back yard, and water balloon battles. Morgan was like champagne, bubbly and a celebration, lots of fun, with lots of friends.

I love one photo collage that hangs in her room. In it, you can see the progression of one particular favorite dress that is worn by a different girl at each event. They hung out together, loved and shared like sisters.

Morgan had so many talents and attributes. She wasn't just a pretty face. She was a great artist, wrote some fine poetry, had a strong work ethic, and she had a compassionate heart, even as a child.

Morgan was a strong student who graduated from Lord Botetourt High School with a 3.93 GPA and was granted early admission to Virginia Tech in 2007.

After the April 16th campus shootings, we thought Morgan would be incredibly safe at Virginia Tech. Who could have ever imagined that college would be the death of her? Morgan was such a homebody. I think she spent every single weekend home with us in Roanoke her first year of college. She liked being home, only a forty minute drive from campus, spending time with us, playing with our new puppy, and catching up with her brother, Alex.

He will be without her the longest. They were supposed to be lifelong friends and companions, but instead, Alex became an only child at 22. Alex was devastated by the loss of his little sister. He grieved in a profound and visceral way. Alex claimed the duvet from Morgan's bed and took it back to his New York apartment to smell and feel and try to conjure her with. That object is small comfort, given that Alex will be the last guy standing in our family. The one with all the inside jokes that no one else understands.

Morgan also participated in several community service projects. For years, Morgan volunteered weekly with Mental Health America's program for children involved with domestic violence. She spent summers helping special need kids at Camp Easter Seals in Craig County.

Morgan frequently packed medical supplies for Orphan Medical Network International, OMNI, and planned to travel with the team to Zambia, Africa, to serve on a mission after her college graduation.

These experiences and the fulfillment they brought Morgan made her decide in 2009 to choose Early Childhood Education as her major at Virginia Tech. She knew she could contribute as a teacher, and she just loved being with kids.

Morgan was not perfect. At one point during her high school years, I was almost running a tab at the Roanoke wreck repair to keep up with all of her fender benders. Our family has always been tightly connected and very loving.

You may get a sense of our relationships and of Morgan's personality from these images and notes of hers:

2008

Mom & Dad,

I feel like we talk so much about many things, like my life at Tech, that it is difficult for me to find meaningful words to give you for Christmas. One thing that I appreciate and value about you is the fact that I can always count on you to help me, no matter what. Mom helps me find gifts for friends (Buddha candles rock!), gives me advice on life and homework, and showers me with love and affection. Even when I was younger you would help me color in pictures for class when my hand became aching. Dad always lends an ear when I have a problem. I thoroughly appreciate this and don't know where I'd be without this help.

Just this year you have really helped me spread my wings and settle into a semi-adult life. Mom, you provided all the furniture and art for my apartment and helped me lug it in! Most kids my age have to scrounge for things to fill their apartments but I was lucky enough to be already set up. Dad, you helped me pick out my apartment, touring each complex and ultimately picking Foxridge. You also help me immensely financially, allowing me to go to school without having to work to pay for rent. Also, you've really helped my friends, and I'm thankful for all you've done for them.

Thank you for all you do for me. I hope you know I appreciate everything.

241

Mogo

Morgan was a talented artist as well as a skilled communicator. Some of her last drawings include "Puzzled Face" and "Eye See the World" both from 2008. I would also like to share some of her school essays as well as messages to family.

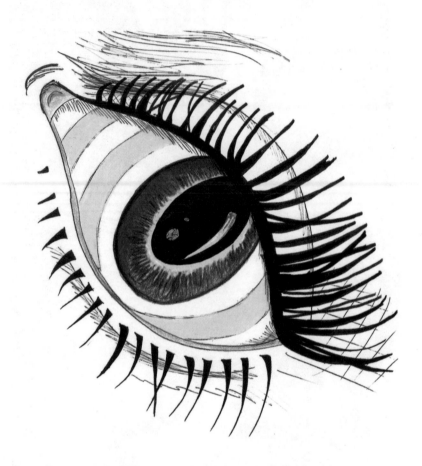

TURN YOUR LIGHT UP!

Revolutionize the mind
Lay down all your pain
get rid of all your hate
It ain't gonna work no more
This world is run by love
and absolutely nothing more

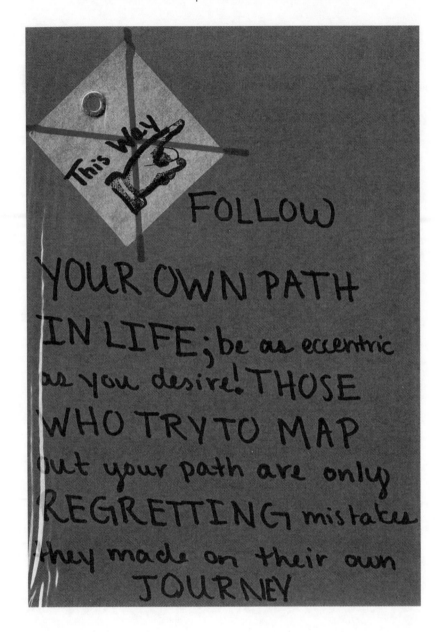

8/2006

Morgan Harrington

Whether or not we want to admit it, we are all products of our parents to some degree. A mother serves as the primary caregiver and influential force in the life of her child. A Father introduces new skills to his child and forms a male role model. Even as children grow up and begin to develop their own ideas and opinions of the world, they maintain the initial foundation, that their parents ~~laid~~ laid in the back of their minds. Although it might sound cliché, the most influential force in my life would ~~undoubtably~~ undoubtably be my mom.

When I was a child, I was constantly in awe of my mother. From her ability to turn any mistake into a blessing to her artistic ~~abilities~~ talents, ~~every~~ every aspect of my mom inspired me. The first time I ~~painted~~ painted it was because I had watched her transform a blank creme canvas into a masterpiece and I wanted to have this same sort of ~~coto~~ power over colors. To this day I have some sort of subconscious tendency to buy all black clothes because ~~that is~~ my mom's entire wardrobe is black.

17

Even as I matured and rebelled as a teenager and did everything possible to step out on my own and shed the concepts my parents had engrained in me, my mom's presence guided me through changing times. She had a way of making all of my friends feel right at home from the moment she met them. From the preppy, sweet smiling girls to the mohawked, grunged-out boys that I seemed to be drawn to in my earlier high school years, my mom welcomed them with nonjudgemental arms. During those rare times when I raised hell and spit out every nasty word I could think of, she remained unshaken. Mom was loving when I wanted a kind word, distant when I needed my space, and consoling when I was ready to be comforted.

A big influential aspect of my mom's life that transferred over to my life is her perspective. My mom is into some very "new age" thought and keeps an open mind to new things. She is unconventional and believes in transmitting positive energy and in the healing power of crystals. I too, have picked up some of this way-of-life and have applied it to my daily life for the better.

2004 - morgan

Courage

Courage is one of the easiest qualities to notice in a person but probably one of the most difficult traits to attain. Personally, I do not believe that we can be born with courage. Instead, it is the product of an individual's life-experiences, personality, character, and hardships endured. Sometimes, people who had no idea of their heroic potential have performed completely random acts of bravery; such events are even considered to be miracles by some. When faced with tragedy, danger, or pressure, people either concede in defeat or rise to the occasion. The majority of people let difficult times beat them into submission, but those who are courageous chose to face their demons; this is simply what distinguishes someone of courage from the weak. When I hear the word courage, I do not envision Hercules with his impressive physique or the 9/11 firefighters emerging from the rubble of the towers. Although these people are certainly courageous, I immediately picture the image of my mom before any other hero. When my mom was faced with her sister's grim diagnosis of cancer, she became the embodiment of audacity.

To fully understand my mom's iron-bond between herself and her sister, Jackie, it is necessary to first explain their childhood. Jackie and my mom grew up in Saudi Arabia with their three other siblings, an alcoholic father, and a less-than-suitable mother. One of their sisters died at an early age, so that left only four children in the White household. In Saudi Arabia, there were few playmates available for my mom, so she depended on Jackie for companionship. Later, the family moved to Charlottesville and all of the kids were shipped off to different boarding schools in Virginia. Since my mom wasn't of the prestigious wealthy class that the majority of her classmates were, most people at St. Ann's refused to acknowledge her. Because of her difficulty growing up in her new surroundings, my mom continued to rely on Jackie as her main stronghold. Many late nights, my mom sneaked out of St. Ann's and drove to visit Jackie when she was especially lonely. Even when my aunt got married and moved to Switzerland, my mom and Jackie still talked on the telephone for hours everyday, ignoring the exorbitant long-distance phone bills. The pair remained best friends throughout their entire lives and, needless to say, Jackie was more of a mother to my mom than their real mom ever was.

Last year, Jackie had complained of feeling sick and lackluster. At first, no one thought twice about it, assuming that she just had a common bug. After the pain in her stomach not only remained, but also worsened, my mom forced Jackie to go to the doctor. The doctor said she was fine, so once again everyone believed that Jackie was okay. Jackie was finally correctly diagnosed with gastric cancer after visiting several doctors - a number of times. By the time the proper diagnosis was made, months of vital time had been wasted and many tumors had already spread throughout her stomach. Sometimes, I ask myself why the doctors couldn't have been more careful, more efficient. Maybe if they had found out earlier, she could have been saved. Over the last year, she shrank to under 80 pounds and virtually lost the ability to eat, go to the bathroom, and even get out of bed. The hardest part for my mom was understanding Jackie's need to raise her two daughters but knowing that Jackie just didn't have enough energy to do much for them; it was like the roles had switched, now Jackie was the child and her kids were suddenly forced to assume responsibility for her. My mom realized that time was running out and she desperately wanted to be with Jackie while she could. She flew to Switzerland several times, even with a broken ankle, and stayed there for a few months each visit. Being a former nurse, my mom took action at the hospital, demanding the doctors to provide the best care possible. She even practically learned to understand a new language just so she could communicate more easily with the hospital staff. My mom spent many nights pacing the floor, reminiscing on old memories with Jackie, and praying. One of the most courageous aspects of my mom's situation was holding her emotions together in order to be strong for Jackie. When Jackie died, my mom was fortunately there and could help Jackie's family cope with the profound loss.

The best thing my mom did for Jackie when she was alive was handling her family. Jackie's two teenage daughters and he husband were in denial, refusing to realize that Jackie was sick. Mom made them realize that they couldn't waste time in showing just how much they cared for Jackie. After Jackie died, my mom made it a priority to share all there was to know about Jackie so that she girls could remember their mother. Sometimes my mom snuggled with Eva, the youngest daughter, when she needed my mom's shoulder to cry on. My mom made Jackie's last few moments special and truly impacted my cousin's lives in a way that no one else could have.

I know my mom is a courageous heroine because of the love and strength she displayed during her time of tragedy. In a way, my mom has been able to come to peace with the situation and become a divine person because of it. For my mom's tremendous courage, I will always look up to her and view her as my role model.

Morgan's Mother's Day Rap

**(Here's a little piece that might soften your contempt of rap…
If not, you can always read it as a poem-haha)**

Hey yous my momma, tha best one in da world
and I'll always be your smilin' baby girl.
Even when I'm old with white streaks in my hair
I'll be lookin' to you for advice and care.

Your wisdom is present in everything you say.
You can even do simplest things in a thoughtful way.
Never cutting' corners or yourself some slack.
Only thing you ask for is a rub of the back.

The sound of your bracelets jinglin' in the air
lets me know that my sweet Mama is near.
Hear a yelp from the kitchen and I'm not surprised
cuz ya always gettin' hurt, can't seem to re-al-ize

that three days of chores can't be jammed into one
without feelin' like your work is never done.
Most people have jobs from nine ta five—
you ain't even got a lunch break, you got that drive!

It pushes you through and helps ya be selfless
without complainin' or ever lookin' helpless!
And as strong as this makes you, it's time to relax
cuz you need a break, so check out these facts:

You are silly
You are pretty
You are smart
You are tough

You make peace
You make brownies
You make up crazy songs
You make dad smile

You help Pipper, Geezer, AJ, Steph
You help basil grow taller
You help me check grammar
You help yourself to bleu cheese

You set the tone
You set the dinner table
You set me up when I fall down
You set your goals high

You don't screen calls
You don't hold grudges
You don't forget about your family
You don't buy bullshit

You hand feed Spiker
You hand me the remote
You hand-make bread
You hand-le problems well

You pick up the house
You pick yourself up by the mipmop straps
You pick up gum when the supply is low
You pick out the positives

You run yourself ragged
You run to answer the phone
You run this household
You run around town all day

So let's make this Mother's Day joyful and great
Since it's a special day for me to demonstrate
how much I respect you and value your life.
Slow down in the kitchen, be careful with the knife!

Momasita, I've got just one more task,
only one more favor of you to ask:
Snuggle up to your girl, your dog, and your man
Unwind with your family—it's a foolproof plan.

2007

I love you too much...
Forever...
And one more time..
Okay

2006 m

Dad,   2005

I want you to know that you are
my hero. You do so much for everyone
else and very little for yourself; it amazes
me how you maintain such a busy
schedule... The other day I got the chance to
listen to you comfort a patient on the
phone. Your attitude was so genuine and
caring; you really wanted the best for
her. I must admit I even felt uplifted!
That is the first time I have ever
really listened to you deal with a
patient in crisis and it really opened my
eyes to see how much of a selfless, kind
man you are. I am proud to be your
daughter, to be associated with such a
dependable and upstanding person makes me

smile. I am Morgan Dana Harrington, and my dad is Dan Harrington :). I could shout it from the rooftops but I don't need to; this whole community already knows what a fine person you are. Thank you for working so hard to give me a good life. Thank you for being gentle and patient, even when we fight. Thank you for helping me feel happier when I was at a low point. Thank you for loving me, mistakes and all ... You are the best dad in the world and I hope you realize how much I care about you.

Merry Christmas!

- Mor💜 -

Morgan Harrington

Psychology

Lord Botetourt High School

2005

Empty Nest Syndrome

"Empty-nest syndrome is a term commonly used for a psychological or emotional condition that can affect a woman around the time that one or more of her children leave home." (Delvin and Webber 1). Although this is not a syndrome usually acknowledged by the medical community, it does affect plenty of parents (Delvin and Webber 3). "This condition is typically more common in women, who are more likely to have had the role of primary carer" ("Empty" 18). Typical symptoms a mom might feel include her being overwhelmed, deep depression, and wondering where her place is now that her focus is gone.

It makes sense that a mom would feel lost once all her children leave home. After all, a mom does spend at least 18 years with her kids and it is probably very difficult to watch them turn into adults. Does this sound familiar: "I'm not your little girl anymore"? Such comments are easy for a young adult to say but difficult for a mom to grasp. Her whole world is shaken when her "baby" leaves the nest, hence the term "empty-nest syndrome." "The grief of empty nest syndrome may be compounded by other life events happening at the same time, including: retirement, redundancy, menopause, and death of a spouse" ("Empty" 7). All of these stressful life factors along with empty nest syndrome can be overwhelming for a mom to experience.

Empty nest syndrome is more prone to impact women in unhappy marital relationships. Once the distraction of a child is gone, a mom is left to see what is truly there in her marriage (Delvin and Webber 27). One couple recalled that when their child left for college, "they sat opposite each other over exquisite candle-lit dinners every night, and could think of nothing to discuss" (Delvin and Webber 30). Sometimes, with a child moving on in his or her life, parents face difficulty in what to do with their own lives.

I that that having a child leave home would be extremely difficult. Although it is the normal, expected thing to happen, that doesn't make the transition any easier. I think the severity of the syndrome would depend on the behavior of the child. For instance, a parent might be relieved if a bratty, argumentative child leaves; however, a mom might be heartbroken if her precious, sweet daughter goes to college. It is all relative to the quality of home life. I chose to write about empty nest syndrome because my brother just left for college and I'll be going in a year and a half. The change wasn't so hard when my brother left because I'm still here. I think that when I leave, though, the impact will be stronger. Still, my parents are happily married and probably are looking forward to being on their own again even though they'll miss me.

Works Cited

Delvin, David and Webber, Christine. "Empty-nest Syndrome." NetDoctor. co.uk. 2005. 14 Feb 2006 <http:www.netdoctor.co.uk/womenshealth/features/ens.htm>.

"Empty Nest Syndrome." Better Health Channel. 2001. 14 Feb 2006 http://www.betterhealth.vic.gov.au/bhcv2/bhcarticles.nsf/pages/Empty_nest_syndrome?OpenDocument.

August 17, 2007

Dear Morgan,

I have wanted to write you for a long time. Morgan from the time you were born you have been special. From birth you were one of the most beautiful and lovely children I had seen. You have grown to become a lovely, talented, and smart young woman.

I have tried to protect you from the hurts and dangers of this world, but as you grow up, you must take good care of yourself. You have a whole world ahead of you and it is full of excitement and new experiences.

As you head to college, I want you to know that you are loved and supported in whatever career you choose to study. You are a very smart, artistically gifted, and beautiful young woman who can do anything you want to do. I know you are betwixt and between. Part of you wants to stay behind and stay small, and another part is ready for adulthood. Morgan, this is an easy choice. Choose adulthood. It gives you the full life that can be yours. You can live where you want, and be what you want, date and marry whom you want, and live life to the fullest.

Morgan, when you go to Virginia Tech, embrace life. Meet new people, join new organizations, and find friends who will be with you, life-long. This is your time to shine and find your wings. Enjoy your time and learn new ways. Grab life with both hands and run with it.

Your life is like one of your paintings; you can create the image and picture that you want. The future is not mapped out and predictable. It has all the possibilities in the universe for you. Let yourself explore life's possibilities. Don't limit yourself.

Remember that you are loved and that I have never wavered in my love and belief in you. When you are married with children you will see what I mean.

Love, Your Dad

—∞—

Morgan, I just wanted to write you something before I left this morning to head back to New York. I miss you, and I miss us. Remember how we used to play upstairs and make tents and be pioneers, or pretend we were in a colonial schoolhouse, or that we were Greek gods or Pokemon figures or Barbies with superpowers, and so many other things. I hope that we can stay that close, friends as well as brother and sister.

Morgan, you have become a beautiful girl, and if you ever need anything, $, a place to crash, a shoulder to cry on, advice, school or otherwise, I have you covered. You are starting something new when you head to Virginia Tech this fall. I hope Tech is a great experience. We have to go to the UVa/ Tech grudge match together this year so we can watch Tech triumph. So my little sister I really love you. Please come and visit me. I will always be ready.

Love, Alex

—⚡—

Dear Alex (aka lil'bro), I'm pretty broke just now so I don't have the funds to get you an Armani suit, a Chanel bag, or a nice used car. I have no idea how to shrink these fabulous gifts into affordable ones, so I've decided to write you a letter.

I'm very proud of the person you've become. When we were little, I remember we used to fuss at family dinners about being seated side by side. Isn't that funny! Now I see you as a fantastic man and I am proud to sit next to you. Know that I love you and am happy that you are growing and finding your way in New York.

You are an exciting person, always surrounded by exciting people, with fabulous dance parties to go to. Every time I am with you I have a blast. So expect me and my friends to visit your cool space often. I hope you realize how much I love you.

241 Mogo

—⚡—

Every parent realizes that children are not perfect and neither is any family, but perfection is not compelling. Imperfections blended into the mix create beauty.

Morgan did the blend superbly. She was beautiful and free-spirited. Morgan always had that gift of integrating apparently disparate items into a whole new look. Definitely eclectic, she wore gold and silver bangles with rubber bands and maybe a couple of buttons on a string. Morgan wore leopard print stilettos, or Birkenstock sandals, and sometimes her red Chucks.

And with all her heart, Morgan loved music. During high school, Morgan traveled to the Algood Music Festival with her friend Erin. The top two items on their list of gear to take camping for a week were hula hoops and a full-length mirror. So it was fortunate that Erin's papa, Tony Cole, was along to handle incidentals, like the tent, water, food, and sleeping bags. Morgan listened to everything, Metallica, the Beatles, Keller Williams, and Bob Marley. She loved the breadth and variety of an unexpected mix. She was really something special, our Morgan.

We are overwhelmed at the unfettered generosity and kindness of our community. Within four days of Morgan's abduction, friends and administrators at the clinic where Dan works gather and add $100,000 to Morgan's reward fund. With Metallica's contribution, we have $150,000. This large reward amount and heavy media attention bring tips and possible sightings pouring into Virginia State Police. Their capacity, like ours, is stretched to the breaking point.

Within days of Morgan's disappearance, someone creates the findmorgan. com website. The online forum on findmorgan.com is intensely active and gains 10,000 followers. A Facebook page is started and quickly registers 33,000 members. Dan spends hours every night perusing investigative theories and chatting with hundreds of folks online, most of whom are supportive and helpful, but some who are quite disturbing.

A ghoulish few come out of the woodwork with visions and premonitions, psychos and psychics. We are open to alternative channels, but cringe at the frankly offensive. I am devastated by the guy who emails me his psychic dream of Morgan's murder. It's a gory pornographic shower snuff script, perverted and awful to read.

For the first time ever, we feel fearful in our home, really aware of locks, and lights, and blinds left open.

We don't want anything bad to get us.

Stupid really: the worst has already happened.

Violent crimes have far-reaching consequences, particularly those which involve our children, our future. Damage is done to the victim, the victim's family, and to the fabric of the entire community.

The response from our friends and community continues to be overwhelming. There are vigils and prayer services, flowers and cakes and cards and casseroles. An astonishing outpouring of love, but still no Morgan.

It has been a week now.

We're tired, getting addled and frayed. We are at the point of snap, that stage where you are so challenged that you may snap and break, or struggle and choose to change and be transformed into new, different, stronger, more flexible and tensile stuff.

At this moment of stretch, bend, and free fall, if you are incredibly determined and creative, triumph is possible.

The fantasy picture I had in mind about how our lives would turn out has been smashed into a thousand pieces. But I can take those shards and rearrange them into a mosaic. It will not be the same picture, not the one I wanted, but if I arrange the memories and our responses to this trauma, can't something somehow still be beautiful?

I know that we must contemplate the possibility of our family becoming a tripod, a threesome, not the solid four-legged table it has been. I have to confront these thoughts and bolster my courage. I instruct my own heart: regardless, we are still a family, and our love is going to sustain us.

I see Dan growing and changing. Amazing, that he can be so strong amidst such anguish. Our worst time has been the time Dan has been the strongest. Like ET, we try to let our heart light shine. We allow ourselves to be vulnerable, open, undefended, to let people see who we are, who Morgan is. We are hoping the beacon of our love will guide her home.

October 28, 2009

And then, triggered by a thought, or a cloud, or the sight of something in the refrigerator Morgan loves, all my optimism suddenly feels frail and poorly built.

Suffering depletes us.

Fear and agony are a churning ocean.

We are drowning in it.

Where will we find the energy we need? There have been 75,000 hits on findmorgan.com, more than we can handle.

And that's exactly when Jason Maloni with Levick Strategic Communications in Washington, D.C., gets in touch with Dan.

Their group does crisis management, and they offer to work pro bono and help us manage a social media effort. Levick is a godsend. It's the first time social media is utilized to assist in a missing person's case, using many platforms, Facebook, Twitter, YouTube, Flickr, and a family blog, to maintain awareness and solicit information and tips in Morgan's case.

Dan is headed back to work, so I am the logical one to do the family blog. Unfortunately I don't know how to type, or use the computer.

Levick says no problem. They arrange for a call-in recorded phone line and make transcriptions magically available to me. I spend time every night in our basement, talking into the phone, streaming my thoughts, streaming to keep from screaming. I end every entry with 241, two four one, our family saying: I love you TOO much, FORever, and ONCE beyond forever. 241 means unconditional love. Those were the last words Morgan said to me, as she adjusted her mirror, eyed her lipstick, smiling, "241, Mama," leaving <u>our</u> home for the last time, October 17, 2009.

Search and Rescue/Recovery

Two weeks after Morgan's abduction, law enforcement asks us to come to Charlottesville, so they can review their search efforts with us. We go to the University of Virginia police station and they give a pretty slick presentation, with maps and charts of the areas they have "cleared." I'm addled and naïve at the time, so I am satisfied.

But Dan is another story.

I watch as irritation and then anger show on his face. Dan says, "Okay, so you have searched the university grounds thoroughly. What about all these other adjacent areas over here, along Routes 29 and 250? Have you searched there?" The message from the police starts to change, to stiffen. Their answer: "We are asking hunters in those areas to be aware in the woods."

We are told that the VSP search policy is to search "only for cause." Which means, that if an item, like Morgan's boot, is found, or a sighting is called into the tip line, VSP will search exactly there.

We are incredulous. Dan and I are really incredulous.

"So essentially, you don't search to find Morgan, but instead you wait and hope she shows up, somehow?"

Apparently so.

In our minds, wait and hope are not a strategy, but that seems to be the policy. VSP say that this limited approach is necessary to preserve resources. At the same time, they will not utilize outside resources like the FBI, because they don't want to relinquish jurisdiction over Morgan's case.

We see the flaw. Can't do it this way, won't do it that way.

Dan and I see the resulting delay suffocating the effort to find Morgan.

Despite our pushing, this policy of waiting to see what unlikely little piece of Morgan a hunter, a dog, or a jogger might find and then bring to the police station remains the stance of VSP.

So we go around them.

Dan calls Ed Smart for advice on how his family orchestrated search efforts when his daughter, Elizabeth, was missing. Ed recommends the help of the Laura Recovery Center and suggests we call to see if they will come to Charlottesville to coordinate a community-wide search for Morgan. He graciously offers to travel to Charlottesville to promote the search effort. I continue to journal.

November 3, 2009   *Scent Bags*

The Laura Recovery Center team will arrive and set up in Charlottesville on Thursday. They were recommended by Ed Smart. It has been difficult, bewildering to determine who we need to help us. The Laura Recovery Center, though, has been invaluable.

I remembered last night that the spot on the bridge where Morgan was last sighted is exactly where a dear friend, Frantz Stilfried, careened off the sidewalk in his wheelchair and tumbled to his death, several years ago. Comforts me somehow to think that he might be looking out for Morgan in that space.

Dan is so fine. Could never go through this without him. We cherish each other so, and that bond is vital in this campaign to find Morgan. Went to Morgan's apartment today to get scent cues for dogs. Took her pillow cases and cut away the fitted sheet from her bed and ziplock-bagged them like it was a surgical sweep. How surreal, those scent bags in Dan's car with flowers and plywood signs to take to Charlottesville in the morning.

241

—∞—

November 5, 2009   *Stumbling*

Driving to Charlottesville—this is crazy. I'm not able to integrate and process data like Dapper Dan does, but trying in my way to use my knowledge and my love to save Morgan. We are struggling, stumbling around like robots. I caught myself trying to unlock my car using my cell phone today.

Dan and I have systematically tried to build such a zone of safety and love around our kids. How could it not be enough? How could it not be enough to keep Morgan safe?

241

—∞—

My dear friend, Karen ReMine, Orphan Medical Network International's President, returns from Zambia, Africa, quite sick with malaria, but she insists on stopping at our house on her way home from the airport. Karen sees Morgan missing in my eyes, and we fall into each other's arms.

Karen is so weak and woozy. I'm pretty wobbly myself. We make a sorrowful pair.

Karen says she will be well enough in two days to participate in the Laura Recovery Search of Charlottesville. I doubt that her rallying is possible. Maybe Karen can come and help with paperwork, instead?

As we prepare to leave for the search, Dan picks up an overnight bag for Morgan, in case she is found. He goes through all of her drawers to find a favorite hoodie and PJs.

"Morgan will need something soft and warm to wear on the way home," he says. That bag becomes a symbol of hope and goes everywhere with us.

The Laura Recovery Center is an amazing machine. They come from Houston, Texas, to Charlottesville, Virginia, with the team of eight, and are able to mobilize and train 2,000 volunteer searchers who work for three days and clear hundreds of acres of land. There is a tremendous outpouring of help from the community, and amazing energy.

Some of the stories I hear make me smile. One volunteer asked a store manager for a donation of bottled water for the searchers. When the manager hesitated, the volunteer said, "Ma'am, if you will help in the search for Morgan Harrington with a donation of water, I will remove the dead skunk from your parking lot that is keeping your customers away." Deal made!

On the second day of the search, I am amazed to see surprisingly elaborate hors d'oeuvres being offered in the snack room. It turns out that a wedding in town was canceled, so the caterer thought of us and brought the wedding cake and all the food to fuel the search.

A coworker of Dan's, Dr. Wayne Gandee, had recently received a challenging cancer diagnosis and was unable to search. But Wayne and his wife, Marianne, were both there anyway, working together, mopping floors and feeding the masses of searchers between shifts, grace and compassion in action.

—⁂—

November 6, 2009   *Jackie*

Why do other people care about this? Ours is not a sanitized, commercialized story, but a raw and painful one, as we navigate the losses that happen to all of us. How can I let my shields down and learn how to show others? I know only the "mama wisdom."

I have had many great teachers. All the mamas who take the cut of meat with the bone in it and make our families believe that it is our favorite part. I remember my sister, Jackie, making pasta sauce as she was dying with cancer and putting it in little containers on the counter. Looking her teenage daughters in the eyes and telling them, "we will put these in the freezer, and after I am dead, there will be home-cooked meals for a while. When you get to the last container, it will not hurt as much."

I have had master teachers. I need them all now.

241

—◊◊—

It is overwhelming to see how generous and compassionate people are. Yes, evil exists, but there is so much good in the world, much more than evil.

Karen ReMine has recovered from malaria and manages to do several runs with the search dog teams. No paperwork for that girl. Dr. Carol Gilbert, who runs a dog search team, some years before saved the life of Dan's brother, Jimmie, when he was crushed by a train. Jimmie's daughter, Julie, comes from Northern Virginia to search for her cousin Morgan and meets Dr. Gilbert. The circularity and connections are staggering.

The search effort demonstrates love in action, but doesn't manage to reveal our girl.

Our community, friends and strangers, lavish caring and compassion on us. Their concern helps us so much. Despite feeling open and raw, we are still able to keep moving forward because we have been carried by so many people and lifted by so many prayers.

—◊◊—

November 7, 2009 Original

People ask me to give one word for Morgan and it's difficult to do. Morgan liked Birkenstocks and platforms and Chucks and didn't see them as mutually exclusive. You can like them all.

Morgan was not a remote princess in an ivory tower. She is a real, beautiful, free-spirited girl, accessible.

We had the responsibility of caring for a rare, precious original. What do you do when you have an original, something genuine and beautiful? You appreciate and love it and look after it, take care of it.

We are devastated and outraged. We tried to protect our own. Protecting our young, that is what parents do. This community is not the anonymous type, one in which people think, "thank God it wasn't my kid," but they think instead that one of OURS has been taken. They are ALL ours. All of our children are precious. We still manage to snatch moments of normal. We will find a way.

241

———※———

November 8, 2009 Roommate

Part of this journey is embracing and being embraced by an ever-expanding circle of family and connections. The pain is profound, but made bearable by the love and support we are bathed with.

Morgan's roommate was here to visit today, and I gave her the funky tie-dyed t-shirt Morgan had chosen for her as a birthday gift.

I am determined to keep the connections and caring and love flowing. I refuse to let the pain ferment and grow, especially in these young, impressionable lives. Enough is enough. It is imperative to me that we limit the collateral damage of Morgan's abduction. We are all hurting, but we can hold each other up and find a new way.

241

———※———

Our relationship with VSP deteriorates. Their voices sound strained after the Laura Recovery Center search, but we are convinced that the vigorous search needed to happen.

More search happens. VSP is not particularly happy when we bring in the maps and say, "With you or around you, we WILL search for Morgan, NOT wait for her."

Karen ReMine becomes passionate about the benefits of using canines to ameliorate the suffering of families with missing loved ones. She joins a canine search team, and participates in multiple searches of likely areas in proximity to Charlottesville, looking for Morgan. Karen eventually obtains a golden retriever puppy to train in the extremely rigorous discipline of search. The pup, Savannah, is named for the wide grasslands in Zambia that reflect her golden-colored hair.

I want to be free not to miss such beautiful reflections and connections.

I want to find Morgan. I want to tell her how hard we searched, and then smile because she is smiling at me, her long golden hair sweet, and clean, and safe, and home.

—⁂—

November 10, 2009 *Angry*

Tired, spent, hitting the wall, but still forcing ourselves to go like robots to get out the message of Morgan. Alex is the only one of us who has had many moments of genuine grief. Afraid if we go there we will drown and not be able to do this job.

We have lavished love on our kids and each other, kisses in the fog of the shower door, notes in the sock drawer. So glad we didn't waste any of the precious time, didn't know it would be so short.

You catch yourself in moments of despair. Like seeing the snack she likes in the cupboard. But you also catch yourself in moments of joy like when the dog comes in dressed in a funny costume. I know we will make it and string these moments of joy and normal together and have a new life. It is difficult, though.

I am starting to get angry. I am slow to anger, but once it takes hold I am relentless. I will tear apart this world to find Morgan and get this guy. If he manages to hide he will still reap his punishment in the next. But I am on the move and I will prevail.

How can it be that our best case scenario is that our daughter is being held against her will? Next best is she is dead. Worst is we will never know and agonize forever. The bag taped shut of her DNA, hair and toothbrush is in her room, next to her baby trunk...with the prints of her starfish-like feet in yellow paint. How has it happened that we are living this schizophrenic, unbelievable kaleidoscope?

241

—⚒—

November 11, 2009   *Raw*

Our intertwined lives are now abraded and raw. Open like a wound. I know that once the skin's protective barrier is breached, infection can grow and fester. Or, we can be like a field, tilled and ready for seeds of next harvest. I choose to plant in the raw space, not bleed.

241

—⚒—

First Holiday Season

These first times of family celebration and festivities are particularly excruciating for us. Our family is broken. We don't really know how to proceed.

Eventually we decide the best strategy is to follow our usual traditions as well as we are able.

Thank God for the generosity of friends. Dan and Alex and I travel to Charlottesville to spend Thanksgiving with the Rives family, as we typically do. We are hideous guests, bolting sporadically from the table in tears whenever the gap at Morgan's place grows large. Their home is a place of sanctuary for us regardless, fireplaces lit, centerpiece of evergreens and driftwood majestic.

Susan was hanging over my hospital bed the day Morgan was born (suggesting both lipstick and morphine). Susan's girls, Amelie and Lizzie, are Morgan's god-sisters. Their family accepts us even in the raw wildness of our pain, loving Morgan and us without reserve.

I think Alex spends the entire Thanksgiving night away from the table, out on the porch with Sandy Rives, our host. The two of them share whiskey and tears in the cold, all evening. Somehow we manage to muddle through the long day and the dreadful night with the strength of their love and support.

November 12, 2009 *Flyers*

How to keep searching and never quit and not burn out in the process? It will take some figuring, I know. But we can do it.

*People today are going to distribute Morgan's missing flyers and bumper stickers at polling places. Brilliant idea. I know from living overseas that women and children are chattel in many lands. America puts a different, more sophisticated face on it. A little more slick, but it is the same here. Look at the month of October, two covers of **People Magazine**: Elizabeth Smart and Jaycee Dugard. Is this a trend?*

What is happening to our world?

I am streaming to keep from screaming. I must become so permeable to the pain of this that it just passes through. Let it pass through me. We are getting more ragged. Dan is losing so much weight he is hitching up his pants constantly. I have to ask Chriss R to go buy better fitting britches. We are forced to have such new intimacies like this with our friends. I am starting to look like a stick with a bun. Even the dog won't eat. We are becoming a family of skeletons. Morgan, are you a skeleton now, too?

241

—⧓—

November 17, 2009 *Learning*

People want a happy ending. The happy ending might not come. Instead what they get might be a take-home message and a modeling of how people can proceed through a tragedy with dignity.

I believe there is a shift as a country towards community. We are seeking and feeling reconnection and intimacy.

I don't know how to do this, though.

We know a surgeon who has had his fingers burned off. He didn't know how to operate with the pads of his digits, but he learned, as we can learn.

I believe there are heroes among us. I am not a Pollyanna. I also recognize that evil exists. The trick is to choose not to let it defeat you. And you do so by living well, not letting this tragedy poison your life. Using your pain to open yourself to others' pain and be more compassionate, make more connections rather than pull away from the world.

Acknowledging and sharing in the joys of your colleagues and friends is what makes life rich and worth living. Holding others up when tragedy hits, as we are being held.

If you let the loss ruin your life, you let the guy who snatched Morgan win. You let evil win. I can not and I will not let that happen.

241

—⸄⸅—

December 3, 2009   *To the one who has Morgan*

Evil shoots popes and presidents and snatches young girls. And those criminals are remembered with scorn. But there are heroes and courage. **Be this.** *I know you want to do the right thing. Things have gotten out of hand. Be remembered as the one who saved Morgan Harrington. Let her go, TODAY.*

Winter holidays are here. We need her home. Please, **please** *let her go.*

241

—⸄⸅—

December 5, 2009   *Darwinian*

It seems we just traveled to Charlottesville for Thanksgiving and visited the bridge to beg for Morgan's release. This country is built on the rule of law where a girl should be able to walk along the street and be okay. That civility is the agreement within our society, so how can we tolerate this Darwinian field where the stronger and bigger conquer, where we see only survival of the fittest?

We are becoming unglued here at home. Angry at fate and each other for not making it all better, yet we have nothing to give to make our predicament okay. I hate to wish the days away, but I hope this one is over soon. December has been a difficult month.

241

—⸄⸅—

December 6, 2009   *Impotent*

How to keep Morgan's voice and presence from being erased from the world? It seems scarier out at night. I don't like the black squares in the windows at night--they seem to be threatening somehow. I go around closing blinds and curtains, switching on lamps.

*It's difficult to be able to help Morgan in any tangible way, so difficult to be...impotent. I am a compulsive nurturer. Having come from little nurturing, I try to give much all around. I am aware of mothering needs to such a degree that I am concerned now about the squirrels in my yard. I haven't been as attentive to the feeders with this crisis, but I make sure to get up and not quit on the struggling wild animals. Winter is coming, and these young creatures need warmth and food and tending. So does **mine**. The young life I was tending. Where is she? Morgan, please come home.*

241

—◊◊—

December 8, 2009   *Puddle*

Morgan missing for so many days. I haven't cooked anything in almost a month besides tea and one batch of scrambled eggs for Alex. Our neighbors and friends continue to lift us up and nourish us. Amazing.

Dan and I often collect beautiful images to share with each other at night. For me, it's easy. I tell him about a beautiful maple tree I saw or something funny that the dog did. Dan is at a disadvantage. He goes to work in the dark. But he shared his impression of the iridescence of an oil-slicked puddle in the parking garage. What a man he is. This is the kind of energy we must harness to become better.

241

—◊◊—

December 9, 2009   *Each month*

This is how you suffer. You sit in the pain and you figure out a way to go on, a path on which to move forward. Try not to redirect the emotion into anger or blame.

I keep asking myself, what is the interest in our story with other folks? I think that audiences have been fed a caricature of behaviors and emotions, which they reject. They seek a more mature stance. They want to figure out how to deal with the inevitable pain life will deliver. Synthesis is tough, though. Thought I could spend the rest of my life underscoring the assumptions and conclusions I had already made, not trying to make new tracks.

Richness is the complexity of your relationships. Each month into our crisis we have received a month of food from the ladies in the neighborhood. That is richness beyond measure.

241

—✺—

December 10, 2009   *Creases*

It's not…it's not getting any easier. The days are heavy with the absence of Morgan from our life. Not sure how to integrate this loss, although we have managed it so far for weeks and weeks and weeks, just breaking things into smaller steps, the next task. I try not to contemplate the next day or the next week. It seems like we have been in a giant farcical game of hide and seek. I want to call, GAME OVER, and get all the players back onto home base. I pray that can still happen.

Dan is getting vertical creases on his face, riverbeds where the tears flow down.

This is so hard.

241

—✺—

December 11. 2009   *Obscenities*

Driving up through our neighborhood, I see all the yellow ribbons displayed for Morgan. It is humbling and heartwarming. Almost every home has a yellow ribbon out somewhere. I noticed that ours are getting tattered from the wind. It has been almost eight weeks, so no wonder.

Dan and I feel like we are tattered, also. Only natural, after so many weeks. We have not started to have time for contemplations and integration of our huge loss. Generally, we do okay. Mornings are better. Later in the day, with fatigue comes vulnerability and fear and such sadness.

Morgan is everywhere in my thoughts. We try to stay in neutral places, like if the TV is on, it's not on the news, maybe a cooking show. But then I get to thinking how I can never pass on to her how to make special recipes or treats we enjoy at Christmas, and then, I'm back in the hole.

45

It's tricky navigating danger areas that might throw you back into the wasteland of despair. They found the body of a young woman in Campbell County this week. They're certain it's not Morgan, but it is someone's precious child, and the magnitude of the loss and the outrage that her life is extinguished is profound. Reading articles about this event with words jumping out at me— decomposed, decapitated, small-framed female—the obscenities rock me on my heels. This is my life now.

241

—∞—

December 12, 2009   *Special child*

I helped pack supplies for Zambia for several hours this week. It was the first time since Morgan was taken that the stone on my heart lightened a bit. Maybe that will be my salvation—finding some healing through helping others. I hope so. Also, I'm in a quandary as to how to mark the Christmas holiday. I don't want to ignore it, but I'm not able to fully participate in joyful celebration just now. How do I honor this holiday that marks the birth of the special child, and at the same time acknowledge the ugly fact that my own special child is not here?

So far, I have been able to put one candle in the window of Morgan's room, and today added a plain fresh wreath with a yellow ribbon on our front door. It feels authentic to me, and it is enough for now.

241

—∞—

December 16, 2009   *Morning*

Morgan Dana Harrington. We gave you the name "Morgan" because it sounded strong, as we wished you to be and to grow to be. It is a name meaning "morning" in German. Beginning, newness of light, dawning of something.

Morgan, my morning girl, we are mourning you. In our darkness, we need your light. Rays of Morgan to dispel this gloom and fear. Find your strength and wisdom and follow the beacon of our love back home.

241

—∞—

December 18, 2009   *Parade*

I find myself several times a day with my breath choppy, caught in my throat. It's a different place for me. Generally, I see myself as being fairly strong and have never experienced episodes of anxiety before. Then I also begin to wonder—if this is a kind of referred feeling—a mother instinct if you will, from Morgan. Is someone choking her and holding back her air? Mentally, I can only touch lightly on the possibilities of what Morgan has gone through or is being subjected to now. It is too difficult to consider for long.

We plan on going to the send-off of the Roanoke Christmas parade to see the Find Morgan Car entry tomorrow night. It's the first big gathering that we will be part of since Morgan was taken. Our grasp on stability is tenuous right now, and I hope we don't get too rattled by the crowd and the parade. We can do it and be strong, I know, just as we are asking Morgan to be strong—strong enough to hold on and to come back home to us.

241

—∿∿—

December 19, 2009   *Shovels*

I thought the yellow ribbons around the neighborhood were sad in the rain—in the snow they are heartbreaking.

Being transparent in this crisis has at times been painful, but has increased our sense of connection with many. Separation is really an illusion, after all. That point was apparent to us today as we attempted to dig out of the 18 inches of snow that has gridlocked our area. We have been pretty overwhelmed with things even before the complications of a major snow storm.

We shoveled our way out of the driveway three times—both Dan and I were exhausted. Dan had fallen twice, while shoveling, and the snow had socked us in again. Faster than we could clear, it piled up. We had quit and given up when some of our neighbors drove up. Folks of all ages piled out. Shovels were lifted and in short order our driveway was clear. The culture of caring in our community really sustains us. This generous kindness shores me up when we are despondent, and renews my belief in goodness and gives me strength to keep hoping that we will find Morgan.

241

—∿∿—

December 21, 2009   *Giving*

I keep ruminating on the concept of giving. We have been given so much during these anguishing weeks since Morgan's disappearance, to an overwhelming and humbling degree. This is different than gifting. Gifting is usually a type of transaction with expectations of getting something in return. Giving is more open-handed and spontaneous it seems, and does not seek reimbursement. Its sole purpose is for contribution and to enhance the richness of connection.

I believe that the practice of giving and generosity is the greatest wealth found in healthy, unified communities. We are grateful to have received this blessing from our community.

241

—⁓—

December 22, 2009   *Participate*

We walked last night with the Forgotten Kids—the forgotten victims from the Mental Health Association—and the Find Morgan Car in the Roanoke Christmas Parade.

We were reluctant to participate—not sure we could hold our fragile sense of coping with all the stimulation of a parade, but we did alright.

So many faces and eyes, it was difficult to process it all. But many prayers and blessings called out. I kept thinking, "We can do this, stand up and be counted and recognized as parents of a missing child, despite the discomfort of being visible."

I saw every mother's and father's face on the route and I read the "thank God I'm not them" look in their eyes. But this was not a turn-aside moment for us. This role was thrust onto us. We did not choose it, nor do we embrace it. But I can certainly find it in me to stand up in the space to be counted and to honor Morgan.

I was struck by the rightness and circularity in walking the parade route in downtown Roanoke. Morgan has walked nearly the exact same route many times, participating in the annual fundraising event for the Roanoke Mental Health Association. Now, some kids who received those services are walking it for Morgan.

As I think of this, I realize it is indeed so fitting. Morgan is now actually one of them—a subject of violence, a weaker being, preyed upon by someone who has run amuck, I believe.

I am grateful for the opportunity to walk the route for Morgan; happy we dug deep and found the strength. It was important to participate.

A friend who worked with the Mental Health Organization reinforced my growing insight on how to cope. Watching her during the parade, her family has just recently been given a difficult cancer diagnosis. And yet, in this time of her own despair, she shows up—hopping up and down with the cold—to bring attention to the ongoing search for Morgan. To lessen the load of despair in our family, rather than to stagnate in her own challenge: that is courage, and that is how you not just survive, but transcend tragedy.

I've learned to use my pain, not succumb to it. And to use it to help an ever-widening circle. Extend your parameters of self to include all—cherish, protect, help all. That will be our salvation.

241

—⚹—

December 23, 2009   Shoes

I have realized that both of us are grieving Morgan's abduction in atypical ways for us. I am usually the more extroverted, expressive person in our relationship and Dan is a bit more shy and reserved. That has been a consistent pattern for almost 30 years, yet in this unbelievable place we find ourselves today, our roles are changing.

I find myself clamming up, looking inward, seeking answers inside. At the same time, I see Dan expressing more, reaching out, more extroverted in his attempts to make sense of our new reality. Maybe this is the growth we are meant to find here. I'm not sure, but I know it adds another layer of discomfort to our feeling of being out of control.

If Morgan's abduction is an event meant to teach us to grow, I think I'm about as big as I can be, or want to be. It is so difficult.

We walk softly around each other, aware that any misstep can break the delicate composure we have built, and expose raw emotions underneath. Despite that care, we still get blindsided easily.

Getting dressed today, I was looking for a particular pair of shoes to wear with some slacks of mine. Of course they aren't here--Morgan has them at school. And so, I started my day already overwhelmed with the loss of, the missing of, the mourning of our Morgan.

241

—⚹—

December 25, 2009   *Christmas Poem*

Our triangulated family
Doesn't have a Christmas tree
It was too hard you see
To contemplate what used to be
All the shattered memory
Couldn't stand the sharp torment
Of baby crafted ornaments

But our home's not Scroogeish or bare
There's still Christmas in the air
With candles and lights and flowers too
Sometimes we cry
But we all try
Strive to create a tradition that's new
Knowing Morgan, that it's true
That your family honors you
By living fully, and so we do

241

—⚏—

Christmas is a replay of the same anguish with a different beloved family, the Hansons. We do sort of okay, until so many sweet little girl faces that Morgan babysat for overwhelm our coping. We end up back on the porch crying, Alex again smoking like a fiend, Dan and I thinking seriously of taking up smoking ourselves.

December 28, 2009   *Cardinal*

The snowfall is beautiful but disturbing—melancholy. Wonder if Morgan is cold—is snow falling on her face—or is her face covered by leaves in a shallow grave being hidden by the snow. I glance out the window and see the crimson blaze of a cardinal at the bird feeder—my heart leaps for a second at the beauty—then I think its feathers look like blood in the snow. Is that what Morgan's blood looks like in the snow? See how the pitfalls are everywhere— even at the birdfeeder.

I try very hard to remain positive and hopeful, to see Morgan coming home. I envision our reunion—feel her body as I hug her tightly. I imagine

Dan's delight as we put her in the car to bring her back home. At times, I can see it so clearly it almost feels real. Other times I consider that Morgan might be loaded onto a gurney—not our car, and brought back to Roanoke—not to our home, but to the Medical Examiner's lab here.

I pray that sorrow is not the end to this crisis.

Morgan 241

—⁓—

Instead of Santa Claus, Virginia State Police come to our house to collect buckle swabs for DNA. I understand the need, and I'm happy to have our information on file to help in identification.

Still, it is pitiful to watch them collect the sample from Dan. He looks so innocent, like a baby bird with his mouth open for the swab, or someone ready to take communion at church, or is he like a chicken stretching his neck for the chopping block?

Dan is getting more fearful. If he doesn't find me quickly by phone, he panics, worried that I have fallen on wet leaves or snow. He sees danger all around.

I see suffering all around. I go into a tizzy over the earthworms covering our driveway after a rain and can't drive into the garage. Afraid of killing and hurting them. Can't stand any more pain.

—⁂—

December 31, 2009   *Snow*

We traveled to Charlottesville to meet with the Virginia State Police. The gathering was tense—everyone involved is just desperate for some break that will bring Morgan home. It is difficult for all of us to be forced to wait for some development. We want more active roles—after all, our quest is to FIND MORGAN, not wait for Morgan. But it seems that just now, waiting is what we must do.

So much snow, we weren't even able to get out at the bridge. We stopped our car in the middle of the road and tossed a pine wreath up onto the giant snow bank that covered the place on Copley Bridge where Morgan was last seen. Driving away, the sight looked more like a funeral than I expected.

The snow worries me. Is she cold? Is her abductor snowed out—or even worse, is he snowed in with her? Cannot go there. I pray for strength to come to all of us.

241

—⁂—

January 1, 2010   *Tacos*

You never know when you will get blindsided by the intense memory of Morgan and it will almost knock you over. She is everywhere for us. Dan was tearful tonight—what a hell of a New Year's—while we were making tacos for dinner, because he knew Morgan would have liked this meal. I too was hit by the memories and, while gathering our plates to use, found myself reflexively picking up four plates, rather than three.

Morgan is not here and we feel the lack acutely, her likes and her dislikes, her personality, her aspirations, her quickness, all integral to the very fabric of our lives. Without Morgan, there are huge gaps, holes in our existence. We are trying not to be swallowed into the void, the emptiness of those holes. Attempting to keep hope alive, we pray we will someday be reunited with our precious daughter, Morgan.

241

—∞—

January 5, 2010   *Three Months*

It has been more than three months since Morgan was abducted. That is a difficult number to contemplate. It encompasses a lot of days, a cold ocean of anguish.

Today, I washed and repacked the change of clothes that Dan carries for Morgan in his car. Handling her clothing and doing such a typical chore as laundry was nice in a way, but I realized that your things, Morgan—they don't really need to be rewashed. I needed to feel like I was doing something for you—to try and conjure you up as I fold your shirt and your pair of socks. I couldn't really fool myself, though.

Yesterday, I visited Morgan's Blacksburg apartment. Her life there was so full, so together. I wonder how long it will take us to put Morgan back together once we find her. I pray we get the chance to figure that one out.

Please God, soon.

241

—∞—

January 6, 2010   *Pretty, blonde girls*

It is disorienting to travel to the fabulous cosmopolitan hive of New York City: so much stimulation and busyness to contend with. Because Morgan is missing, there is also an aspect of discomfort when I am reminded just how big the world is—how can we find a needle in this huge haystack? Somehow, we must. I cannot contemplate a world without her.

Many times each day my heart leaps reflexively at glimpses of pretty blonde girls on the street—could it be Morgan? Then they turn their head and the face is different. I cannot help looking at them with hunger.

Being apart from Dan on this trip has also been hard for both of us. We rely on the assurance and constancy of our relationship for sustenance. I feel unmoored without Dan near me. The sacrifice of this separation was necessary though to shore up our remaining child. We always have, and will continue to sacrifice whatever is necessary, to help both Morgan and Alex.

Alex has been hit just as hard as we have and doesn't have a foundational relationship to draw on like Dan and I have together. Still, the devotion of a parent toward a child is phenomenally strong and provides a core of certainty that can be drawn on when life proves difficult. Morgan, you have our unending devotion—draw from this strength to find a way home.

241

—⟶—

January 7, 2010   *Under*

Not sure how Dan continues to function at such a high level. He processes so much information and stays so calm and strong while collapsing inside. The crisis of Morgan's abduction has been so hard on both of us. You brace yourself for possible, inevitable life events so as to better withstand the impact, but we never saw this one coming, never had a chance to brace ourselves. We try to hold each other up—damage control is vital.

I want to limit the injury and hurt that Morgan's abduction has caused. So many lives have been impacted—our family, of course, and many, many beyond that. I will try to pull as many as I can under my umbrella and protect them, try to lessen the pain for all.

241

—⟶—

January 8, 2010   *Masking tape*

Our pain was sharpened by expectations for this holiday season. I found Christmas compromises that were acceptable to me. It was challenging to have a new, different tradition that acknowledges Christmas, and still honors our missing Morgan.

Our décor was pretty muted, but what has been done is genuine and celebratory of love and caring. It's challenging, though, to find that path. Every time I go into our closet, Morgan's gift reproaches me from the top shelf. And then despair almost takes me out.

There have been a couple of smiles that I refer back to, to lift myself. Thinking today about our friend Glen who put masking tape all over his Corvette to drive it in the Christmas Parade as the Find Morgan entry. What a selfless kindness that was. I like to think about people's sweet offerings and remember that, despite everything, we are so blessed.

241

———

January 20, 2010   *Washington, D.C.*

Dan and I are invited to go to Washington, D.C., to lobby Congress in support of the National Center for Missing Adults, CMA, who have applied for Finn federal funding. Marc Klaas is part of their group, and another lobbyist is there, a woman whose mother has been missing since 1998. The missing woman's daughter looking whipped and pinned to a corner under the Capitol dome is telling us about her missing parent. This is rough stuff, and by the suffering I am seeing, the pain never gets better.

    I'm amazed at how accessible and kind the legislators are. We meet with senators Mark Warner and Jim Webb. I give Senator Webb a photograph of Morgan hugging him in her AP history class at Lord Botetourt High School. He blanches when I say, "Senator Webb, you held that girl, our daughter Morgan. I want to do that again."

Representative Bob Goodlatte is genuine and caring and so compassionate. He listens hard and wants to help us. The trip and our new reality is like trying to drink from a fire hose. It's overwhelming.

241

———

January 20, 2010   Before and After

Are we not sophisticated enough as a society that women do not need to walk the streets and be regarded as, treated as, prey? How is this danger tolerated as the price of being female in America? This phenomenon of snatching people is not as common in other civilized countries. Why here? Perhaps because we prize the rights of individuals so much that the collective allegiance fundamental to a group dynamic, requiring social respect and reciprocity, is missing here. So it is each man for himself, do what you want, take what you want—including women and children. They are only stuff after all. This attitude must change. It changes only through cultivating connections and relationships and creating community with expectations of integrity.

56

We are all learning and attempting to awaken and strengthen community even in the face of the crime against Morgan. This is a watershed event for our family. Everything that has happened and will happen to us will be placed in time before or after Morgan was stolen. We will be defined by it, but not by the loss and the pain—instead, by the love we received and gave and the strength we found to continue unceasingly, relentlessly searching for Morgan.

241

—⚊—

Relationship with Virginia State Police

The Virginia State Police are tough cookies. It is difficult for me to connect with them. I think it's because they actually don't know how to connect with victims' families. I don't get that deficit or disinclination. The agent with whom we had felt some rapport, John Phillips, has been reassigned. Special agent Dino Cappuzzo is now our contact person with Virginia State Police for Morgan's investigation. In my meetings with law enforcement, I stress that times have changed, and that we need to find a more interactive relationship.

We, victims' families, want and deserve a role in the process, and Dan and I certainly want to contribute and participate. I point out that only a few years ago, fathers were banished from participating in their children's birth, and instead were relegated to pacing hospital corridors, smoking cigars, and wringing their hands. In today's more informed and inclusive world, Papas are present in the operating room and cutting the umbilical cords of their children. Surely these fathers are not obstetricians, but they do have a role in the proceedings.

We believe that similarly, victims' families are entitled to a role in the investigative process. No, we are not investigators, but by golly we have a role. This is our daughter, our case, as much as it is VSP's case.

They disagree.

I believe they are afraid that any kind of empathy or intimacy would erode their ability to investigate objectively. I keep trying to team-build with VSP, but with little success. At my insistence, we meet regularly, but they consistently and determinedly keep us at arm's length. I can't break through their barriers.

By January, our relationship has grown strained. Nevertheless, we present a united front with law enforcement publicly and address any problems behind closed doors. It's not right to rap their knuckles in the media publicly. For better or for worse, we are yoked together like a marriage, like a family, and will work together and make the best of our bond.

I won't throw anyone under the bus. There will be no collateral damage.

It is a hard position to maintain. I have a growing awareness and concern about an emerging strategy I sense with law enforcement, to protect reputation first, and limit liability by pointing the finger of blame at Morgan. For example? "Charlottesville is safe and Morgan Harrington made herself vulnerable."

Okay, I think, if it's so safe, what was Morgan vulnerable to? Abduction by a predator at the top of his game--that's what. The stated and the tacit message is: don't worry, Charlottesville. You're okay, Charlottesville. There's no danger, no bad guy here, just another bad girl--asking for it. My anger flares at the UVA law enforcement officer who tells us "even a minister would've stopped on that bridge and picked up a girl wearing a miniskirt and boots."

Flabbergasted, I respond, "Are you kidding? Have you been to the mall? Morgan was wearing leggings, a miniskirt, a t-shirt, a jacket, and boots. She was well-covered. In fact, the only skin she had hanging out was her beautiful face. What do you recommend, a burqa? It's not about finding blame; it's about finding our daughter, Morgan."

I'm beginning to stew about the obvious official desire to preserve complacency and reputation, despite the evident risk to the community and to the university that is clear to both Dan and me. We both attended the University of Virginia and love Charlottesville. It is not our intention or desire to trash either one, only to urge caution and prudence. There is a predator walking through the prestigious grounds. Please, you must be alert to stay safe!

Months after Morgan's abduction, in one of our frequent law enforcement meetings, VSP shares with us that Morgan's Pantera t-shirt was found, at the intersection of 15th and Grady Street in Charlottesville, back in November, 2009, about two weeks after the concert.

Her shirt had been draped like a trophy on a bush near fraternity row.

The discovery of Morgan's shirt was not been released to the public.

I am dumbfounded.

I start rioting behind the scenes with Virginia State Police: "I implore, you must alert the community. This predator is so comfortable that he places the most recognizable item from Morgan's abduction right where hundreds of students pass every day."

"This is frightening," I urge. "Please, tell the community."

Their response? "No. We cannot release this information. We want to preserve the integrity of the prosecution."

I beg, "Forget that. It's too late for Morgan. You have a responsibility to this community and to the students walking on the streets. These are your constituents. For God's sake, you've got to tell them that he was here, feeling bold. Urge caution. Please, help save the next girl."

—⚬—

January 24, 2010   *Three Months*

3 months! Despite the length of time Morgan has been gone, I remain hopeful. Part of me is waiting to be surprised. Waiting for God to pull the rabbit out of the hat and bring Morgan home.

I remember that the light always returns. It cannot help but return. Will the light of my life return soon? I cannot imagine that all the water of Morgan's potential is to run down the drain and be wasted. Can it really play out like that?

Come home soon baby.

241

—⚬—

The Missing Phase

MISSING

www.FindMorgan.com

Morgan Dana Harrington

Age – *20*
Eyes – *Blue*
Hair – *Blonde*
Height – *5′ 6″*
Weight – *120 lbs.*
LAST SEEN –
October 17, 2009 at John Paul Jones Arena in Charlottesville, VA

Morgan Dana Harrington, a 20-year-old student from Virginia Tech, was last seen Saturday near the John Paul Jones Arena. The arena was the site of a Metallica concert the night she went missing.

Harrington was last seen wearing a black t-shirt with "Pantera" across the front, a black mini-skirt with black tights and knee-high black boots. She has long blonde hair and blue eyes.

If you have information, please call:

24-Hour Tip Line
434-352-3467

Crime Stoppers
434-977-4000

Crime Stoppers & Metallica
REWARD $150,000

The anguish of not knowing is debilitating. It takes tremendous energy to brace for bad news and to maintain hope at the same time. The effect of doing this double-emotional seesaw plus our media activity is making us ragged. The way I try to manage is to become so permeable to the pain that it just passes through me like a wave.

I'm afraid if I can't do this mind mastery, I will drown in pain. If I can't figure out how to release the pain, transfer it out, it will consume and destroy me.

We all process despair and anguish differently and we must learn how to accept these different grief styles in each other. Typically, Dan and I sustain and replenish each other, but we have no extra to give in the agony following Morgan's abduction. We both feel isolated, alone.

I check deliberately, and Dan's face is actually creased with the grooves from so many tears. In our 30+ years together, I have seen Dan cry only a couple of times before. It disturbs me so to watch now, but I can't comfort him. I am empty.

I have nothing to give. I have nothing to say that makes it better. I cannot change this ugly reality. For me, the hideous limbo of "missing" is beyond tears. I cry only a few times, and those times are extreme episodes of primitive, on-the-floor keening. It's not cathartic: the agonized howls leave me spent and debilitated for days.

One of my worst ugly cry episodes is when Dan and Alex and I go to Morgan's apartment in Blacksburg for the first time. It's a Thursday, just a few days after Morgan's abduction from JPJ in Charlottesville. The apartment has been sealed with yellow police tape--it's a homicide investigation, after all.

Two police officers meet us there to check for any possible evidence in the apartment, and to take possession of Morgan's computer for evaluation. As soon as the door is opened, I am like a crazy woman, moving from room to room, shrieking, and sobbing hysterically, "Look! Look! She had a life! She had such a fine life! She was so alive!"

The three of us swarm over the apartment, wanting to put our hands on every single tiny detail of Morgan's life, hoping somehow to feel her there, find her. Sobbing, we smell her shampoo, touch her make up, and even check the food in the fridge. What was she eating?

We wail when we discover her Halloween costume in the closet. I am a little embarrassed that the two policemen see us acting so bizarre, but no way can we hold back this avalanche of emotion. Her home, her jarring absence, is so awful and sad.

Alex eventually pulls us from the vortex of anguish when he points out: "Hey Mom. Morgan has so many clothes that the closet pole is bending off the wall!" This makes us all smile to realize.

Yes, Morgan had so much, so many things, brains, looks, friends, but no damn luck.

Where is she? Who snatched our Morgan?

If even one tiny circumstance had been different on October 17, then we would have Morgan here with us today. One extra wait at a stoplight, five more minutes before she went to the bathroom, one less predator on grounds. So frustrating to contemplate, but not helpful to dwell on. This line of thinking erodes our forward motion. We must struggle to transcend the agony we find ourselves in.

MOGO

You are missing and I'm missing you
What a horror we're going through
You are missing, but not by choice
Have ta call your cell phone just to hear your voice
And you say "I'll get back to you as fast as I can"
But you never come back to me and Dan
And we're going down the drain, such pain
How can it be?
We've become a family of three

241

Neighbors

I constantly remind myself that love is greater than fear, and I fight dozens, hundreds of times a day to prevent myself from slipping into anxiety and paranoia. It's tricky to manage. I start into the grocery store and get as far as the cereal aisle with my cart, then I see the brand of cereal Morgan particularly liked and I panic. I start hyperventilating and have to leave the store. I try to calm myself in the parking lot. Sometimes I can find the strength to go back inside and actually finish the marketing. Often, not. I am barely functional for even the simple little tasks.

Thank goodness for our community and our neighbors. They have lavished their support and caring on us, so many dinners, flowers, cards, and candle vigils. We drive into our neighborhood late one night and from the entrance of our subdivision up the hill to our home the entire road is lit with hundreds of votive candles.

The light is breathtakingly beautiful and mitigates the fear that darkness brings. It is humbling and so comforting to receive this rich outpouring of love. This constant blessing teaches us how to survive.

Our Bentley Park neighborhood really goes all out to support us. The southern women's casserole brigade is a force of nature, amazing to behold. Any challenge, any loved one in need, sets off a cascade of generosity. Death in the family? New baby? Folks laid up sick? The neighbor ladies take charge and provide Grace in the form of casserole comfort food. It is wonderful when you're too anguished to choke down meals or prepare food to be able to open your fridge to a library of home-cooked food.

The Bentley ladies slipped a note under our door shortly after Morgan was missing: "We are taking over the feeding of your family. You all focus on finding strength to find your Morgan. Here is the menu for this week. Let us know if you have any preferences or allergies, and we can adjust. Dinner will be delivered to your kitchen counter by 5 p.m. every evening."

These wonderful ladies provided daily meals for us from October until after the New Year. Even at that point, I had a little tussle to convince them I was finally strong enough to take over this domestic task. Really beautiful.

People were tremendously supportive, but occasionally there would be an outrageous or baffling comment. We started to keep a list: "What not to say to the parents of a missing girl."

1. Are you OK? Most marriages won't survive such a tragedy.

2. "I have also had some recent challenges. My cat was sick last week."

3. "I know just how you feel. My daughter lost cell phone reception yesterday. I couldn't reach her by phone for 30 minutes. It was terrible."

4. "You look like hell."

5. "Are you the mother of the dead girl?"

6. "I am praying your daughter is being held captive." (I didn't answer this one, but thought, please pray for release instead.)

7. "You can have another child." (I'm thinking, my uterus is in a jar in Carilion Hospital. This is a non-viable option.)

Still, I realize people mean well, but the awkward deliveries unsettle.

Copley Bridge

Love and hope diminish fear and pain. I notice.

I notice even the slightest modulation. I want to be an alchemist, able to stop the pain, the nightmare, to dispel the dark gaping throat of another day which devours us with anguish.

I am trying to command the fear to recede, to become only an ugly background noise, not this violent screaming in my ears. My most crazy-making stimulation isn't auditory, though. It's visual.

Many, many people send flowers to our home. I remember the October/November arrangements. After a few weeks, so much orange and so much floral in the house started to make me anxious, jangled my nerves. I couldn't process beauty anymore. Our home felt like a mortuary.

My protective heart confronted the flowers. I wanted to say to the arrangements, Morgan is NOT dead.

Then I had an inspiration. Let's take them all, this whole lot of chrysanthemums and daisies and carnations and sunflowers, to Morgan's bridge in Charlottesville.

Immediately after Morgan's abduction, Dan and I had started to hold Q & A sessions with media on the Copley Bridge which is close, within a minute's walk, from the JPJ concert arena. This bridge was the last place Morgan was seen outside the arena.

It was also the last place Morgan stood of her own volition, and therefore a meaningful location to us personally. The bridge is also an important place for us to solicit investigative tips for police. "Did you see Morgan here on this bridge on October 17, 2009? Did you see her get into a car here? What model car was it?"

The bridge remains a critical place for us to urge caution in the university community. "A top-tier criminal, a predator stalked and snatched a girl from this very spot. He is still out there, waiting for another chance. Be careful. Please. Let there be no more innocent lives taken."

Dan and I bundle flowers and candles and cards into our car and anoint the bridge in Charlottesville. The display grows organically. Friends, students, strangers, all leave memorabilia, notes, flowers, photos, shells, ribbons, drawings.

A Find Morgan Facebook thread called "Morgan Rocks" brings stones from across the United States and beyond to Charlottesville, Virginia. A friend, Barb, opens a post office box to accommodate the influx of weathered river stones, etched and carved memorial granites, intricately painted bejeweled dazzlers, all delivered to Morgan's bridge as tribute.

The bridge becomes something to see.

Tibetan prayer flags flying, stone cairns stacked amid solar candles, even a glow-in-the-dark cross turns up one day.

The shrine is impossible to ignore.

If you dropped from Mars and saw Morgan's Bridge at JPJ, you would turn your alien head and know that something of note had happened there.

To our family, life as we knew it ended on that bridge, and our life of pain started there. That little arched bridge over the railroad tracks becomes Morgan's Bridge. It has grown into a kind of sacred space, more than a collection of rocks and flowers and flags.

We cannot erase the pain.

I decide: we will learn to manage it, mute it.

The strength to do the necessary work comes directly from the compassion we receive. In continuing the cycle of grace, I begin to see that we may forge our own survival.

I believe in redemption through service and I find solace in this insight, but the pendulum swing of my emotions is still wild and erratic.

It's hard not to be sucked back into despair. It's cold now, winter, and we have had a lot of snow. I wonder again if Morgan is cold. Does he have her chained? Is Morgan tied in a shed somewhere? Or is her face covered by leaves in the shallow grave I never quite allow myself to visualize?

I am trying so hard to hope, to conjure, to pull Morgan back from the universe. I need my girl. Without her, it hurts to breathe.

At the same time, I'm a strong, practical woman, who loves fiercely, even unselfishly.

I love my daughter. Almost unbelievably, I notice an internal miracle. My abiding love for my precious daughter, Morgan, pushes me to release her.

I think a soul has some choice.

In my heart talk with Morgan, I tell her: "Darling, if you are in a spot that is so hard for you that you believe checking out is your best option, Morgan, then go. I will respect your choice. I release you from all the pain of this earth and we will carry the pain from now on. I release you. Fly if you must."

The missing time is so difficult. It is, again and again, like a cruel Escher path turning upside down and redrawing itself, riddled with conflicting emotions, hope, despair, and horror.

My blessing is that as I experience this agony, I am aware that the rock of suffering contains the precious gem of grace with its many facets and brilliant colors.

Response and Synthesis

Part II

Body Found

On January 26, 2010, after Morgan has been missing for 101 days, Dan gets a midmorning call from a reporter in Charlottesville, who asks: "Do you have a statement to make regarding the discovery of Morgan's remains today?"

Dan says, "I don't know what you're talking about. We haven't heard anything from Virginia State Police."

Dan rushes home from the hospital and I start throwing clothes into a suitcase. We finally get through to VSP, and yes, a body has been found this morning, and it's likely to be Morgan's. They tell us to meet at the Virginia State Police headquarters in Charlottesville and they will share their findings.

It a madhouse at police headquarters, media clamoring.

We are ushered into a room and sit around a big conference table. We are told it is almost certainly Morgan who has been found, five miles outside of Charlottesville on a large property called Anchorage Farm.

They are in the process of removing Morgan's remains to be sent to the Medical Examiner's office in Richmond, and we are encouraged to return to Roanoke. Simple as that.

No way.

We are not leaving.

I want to go and see where my daughter's body was abandoned.

I say from the most profound and clear place of my heart: "I want to go there and know the place. This is my duty and my absolute right as a parent. I must go there."

The investigators push back, telling us, "No, you should just remember Morgan as she was. A crime scene is ugly. It's better you don't see."

Dan snaps. "Listen, I'm a physician. I have seen and worked with cadavers. We want to see Morgan on Anchorage Farm."

They won't budge. At this point I am almost ready to blow a gasket. I actually stand up and say, "I'm going to Anchorage Farm. To stop me, you will have to physically carry me away and I'll be kicking and screaming as I go. It ain't gonna be pretty, and I guarantee you that your restraining me will make the news."

Some of the calmer heads around the table, like Jim Mooney from the Charlottesville Police Department, intervene and suggest everyone step away for a break. Twenty minutes later, we reconvene at the conference table and a compromise is offered. VSP will show us some of the crime scene photos, and they will fly us over the body site in a helicopter, if we agree not to go to Anchorage Farm on our own.

The photos are tragic. It is our Morgan. I see her bracelet on black and rotted wrist. Yes, our precious girl is now carrion.

The helicopter ride is surreal. Such an expansive land. I'm struck by how unlikely it is that you were found, Morgan.

There's a big snow coming tomorrow. You would have been hidden forever.

From high up above that fallow field and the surrounding forested mountains and hundreds of rural acres, I see something the helicopter pilot can't know he is showing me, and from my soul, I whisper my discovery to Morgan, wherever she is: you wanted to be found.

You wanted to be found.

Somehow, I know now: eventually, we are going to learn the truth.

It's as close to a conversation as we've had in three months, Morgan's bones down there conveying to mine.

The truth will out.

—⁓—

January 26, 2010   *Bridge Statement*

On the Copely Bridge, facing a swarm of cameras absorbing what will become the forthcoming evening news, I deliver this statement:

Our sorrow is etched on our faces. Our pain is carved in our hearts. But there are stirrings, thankful tendrils of peace growing in our souls.

For the first time in 101 days, we know where our daughter is. For the first time in 101 days, I am not thinking constantly, what is he doing to her now?

It is evident from the condition of Morgan's body that she has been at peace for some time. We draw comfort from that fact. And I can tell you, having seen, that she even had lovely bones.

Please remain vigilant. There is a violent predator in our community. I reject the idea that sexual assault is a regrettable but inevitable consequence of college attendance.

Know your neighbors. Participate in your community. Look out for one another. Together, we can help save the next girl.

—⁓—

January 31, 2010   *Bruises*

Clouds were mottled, purple bruises over the Blue Ridge as we drove over Afton Mountain to reclaim the skeletonized remains of our precious daughter, Morgan Dana Harrington.

We had tried to prepare ourselves for this eventuality for three months, but the reality of it is sharp and disorienting. How could someone have erased so much of what Morgan was and reduced her to a jumbled heap of bones? What a waste, what a desecration, a gross injustice.

Who would have ever thought it would be mine to see every image of Morgan's life—from her first faint shadows on fetal ultrasound to the gaping orbital hollows in her skull? An abomination, to witness this ending.

And yet there is growing peace. We realize Morgan has been dead since the day of the concert, October 17, 2009. Morgan Dana Harrington has been at peace, beyond pain and suffering. Knowing that brings us some peace also.

Once her body is restored to us and put to rest, we can finally begin the hard work of grieving and growing strong as a triangulated family .Bless all of you who have held us up on this journey. My Darling Morgan!

241

—⚬—

Some days after, I wrote:

FROM ME TO YOU/THEN YOU TO ME/JEWELRY

They gave me your bracelet back
Tarnished now, rusty and black
It's the one I had as a girl
It's the one you wore as you left this world
The one that witnessed mortal harm
I'm wearing now on my arm
And I do so with sorrow and with pride
Having seen your desiccated flesh inside
Knowing you wore it as you died.
I have scrubbed it out repeatedly
Since it was returned to me
But still I can tell
It harbors a smell
Of flesh and of rot

But it's all that I've got
And as long as it smells, you can't be forgot

241

—⁓—

Funeral Ceremony

It's not until early February, 2010, that Morgan's body is released by the Medical Examiner in Richmond.

Our neighbor, Allen Simpson, is the funeral director we choose for the sad work of retrieving Morgan's remains from Richmond. It is late when he gets back to Roanoke with Morgan's body, but before proceeding to the Simpson Funeral Home, Allen drives into the neighborhood and parks in front of our house. He opens all the windows of his vehicle. We like to think that some vestige of Morgan's spirit returned to our home that night.

February 1, 2010   *She Mattered*

The world has lost its best hugger. The incomparable Morgan Dana Harrington was torn from us on October 17, 2009.

Morgan, age 20, was a shiny, loving, beautiful original. She was very much loved by her family, her friends, and her community, which has now expanded to include much of the world. We cherish the time we had with Morgan and are grateful for the breadth and variety of experiences we were able to share in her tragically abbreviated life.

Morgan was born on July 24, 1989, in Charlottesville, Virginia, and killed there in October, 2009. She was an avid music fan, a champion of children's rights, and she planned a career in education.

241

—⁓—

Allen makes it possible for us to have a "visitation" with Morgan's remains. It is incredibly sad to realize that this pick-up sticks jumble of ribs and vertebrae is what is left of our vibrant, precious Morgan.

Dan and I are both enraged to see the fractures of her arm and ribs. It is ludicrous really to focus on those discrete areas of damage when the abomination of Morgan's entire skeleton rests before us.

The mind can accept only so much atrocity as it tries to cope and process. We focus on the radial fracture because we can comprehend only that much.

Morgan is cremated. Her ashes are surprisingly heavy. Her bones were strong and dense because she was murdered when she was only 20 years old.

We put Morgan's cremains in her grandfather's cigar box. Even as a child, Morgan had loved to place jewelry and shiny things in that box.

Now, our shiny treasure, our out-of-the-box-girl, is inside the box. Unbelievable.

With Morgan cremated, Dan and I begin to plan her funeral. A sudden winter storm blankets the entire region with deep snow.

Nevertheless, hundreds brave the roads and attend Morgan's funeral mass at Saint Andrew's Church. Father Steve McNally conducts a remarkable and moving service. The beauty and richness of the ritual and music comfort us more than I ever expected.

My Funeral Remarks:

I believe that it takes a soul a little while to find its way to heaven. Especially in a case like Morgan's, where the individual has not been honored, or the body put to rest.

Morgan, in the 101 days your spirit was betwixt and between, waiting to be found, you have taken us on a wild and incomprehensible journey. And wherever you led us, we willingly followed.

You took us to places we have never been, from Capitol Hill to Dr. Phil, and everywhere inbetween. You had us marching in the Christmas parade with the forgotten victims. Morgan, we went to a heavy metal concert hosted by some sweet young men.

You have gotten your Papa on Facebook, and me writing a blog. Who could have imagined such things?

Morgan, you had us flying in a helicopter over the fields of Albemarle County, trying to find you. In the next few days, you'll lead Alex and me to get a tattoo! Dan isn't thrilled about ink, but agrees that the Sharpie marker version is nice.

We have tried to keep our finger off the nozzle and let your blessings and surprises rain down on us, holding fear and doubt in check and moving forward. We will continue to do this.

But darling Morgan, Mom and Dad are a little tired right now. Give us a couple of weeks and then I won't be surprised to find us strapped into the space shuttle on our way to dance with you on the moon, and baby we will go for it!

241

—ɷ—

Following Morgan's funeral, the reception at Hotel Roanoke is amazing. The Crystal Ballroom is full of friends and sadness and joy, even a bubble machine! It is a genuine celebration of Morgan's short life.

We feel it is important to mark the day in a big way because Morgan will not have any of those other anticipated celebrations to mark life's grand moments, no next Christmas, no 21st birthday, engagement, graduation, wedding, baby shower...

A Mother's Thoughts / Not Missing

Morgan
Not missing but found
dead on the ground
No loved ones near
You perished in violence and fear
How can it be
That your destiny
was to be torn from Papa and me
Such an unbelievable fate
Our child of light
extinguishing by hate
Never mother or wife
A tragically abbreviated life
Part of me
would reject Deity
that allowed such atrocity
But know that we
Must surrender to the incomprehensibility
Of mystery
Somehow this is how it had to be

Celebrating the Life of

Morgan Dana Harrington

July 24, 1989

October 2009

Funeral Mass
St. Andrews Catholic Church
3:30pm
Friday, February 5, 2010

Officiating
Father Steve McNally
Rev. Dan Holloway

Reconfigured Family
Dan, Gil and Alex Harrington

The Family will Have a Private Scattering of the Ashes at Unity of Roanoke Valley

The world has lost its best hugger. The incomparable Morgan Dana Harrington was torn from us on October 17, 2009. Morgan, age 20, was a shiny, loving, beautiful original. She was very much loved by her family, her friends, and her community, which has now expanded to include much of the world. We cherish the time we had with Morgan and are grateful for the breadth and variety of experiences we were able to share in her tragically abbreviated life.

Morgan was born on July 24, 1989 in Charlottesville, Virginia and died there in October 2009. She was an avid music fan, a champion of children's rights, and planned a career in education.

To recognize some of Morgan's passions we ask that, in lieu of flowers, gifts to honor Morgan's memory be made to the Morgan Dana Harrington Memorial Scholarship at the Virginia Tech Carilion School of Medicine or to OMNI Orphan Medical Network International, an organization that provides medical care in Africa. Scholarship donations may be mailed to : Virginia Tech, Attn: Gift Accounting, University Development (0336) Blacksburg, Virginia 24061, and OMNI donations to 6930 Empire Lane Roanoke, Virginia 24018. We are grief stricken by her death but also lifted by the knowledge that Morgan Dana Harrington was precious to so many and will not be forgotten. She mattered to us all.

February 14, 2010   *Just Say No*

Won't participate
In a storm of hate
With such negativity
I become the same as he
Who caused this atrocity
Instead, I'll focus on love and not stop
Coz in the end I know love'll come out on top

241

—〰—

February 17, 2010   *Empty*

My obscenity-riddled to-do list has included words such as <u>victim, scent item, fingerprints, DNA, skeletonized, cadaver dog</u>, and <u>medical examiner</u>. Now I add the words, <u>view remains</u>. And that's just what Morgan has been reduced to—calcified fragments.

All he left us with was her bones—but they are precious to us. It is a primal emotion to get the body back to mourn and to honor the life that was lost.

We honored Morgan to the best of our abilities with a moving funeral Mass and celebration of Morgan's brief life.

We mourned Morgan to the best of our abilities by viewing with clarity her cast-off bones, holding her in our own hands in this form as part of our leave-taking. Holding the last remnants of our girl, to try and let the enormity and finality of her death penetrate somehow past the barriers in our minds that still scream, "How can this be? It isn't happening." Peering into Morgan's empty orbital sockets, the mind protests—but must concede, it is. Not an exercise in reality I ever want again to come to me.

241

—〰—

February 22, 2010   *Windows*

I loved it that our friend/neighbor/funeral director personally retrieved Morgan's remains from the Medical Examiner in Richmond. He told me with such kindness about how, when they had arrived in Roanoke, he drove to our home and parked outside and opened the vehicle's windows to allow Morgan's spirit to return home. I am still so moved by Allen's story.

Our community has been so responsive. Our neighborhood has been festooned with a semaphore of supportive ribbons: first yellow to bring Morgan home and keep hope alive, and once it was clear she was not alive, changing to black. Now that she is here and honored, I have taken those ribbons down and left one Spring-colored green ribbon on our elm tree to show that we are capable of, and intend to grow through this experience.

Formula for survival = love more than you fear or hurt and eventually love will prevail. 241

Red Bag

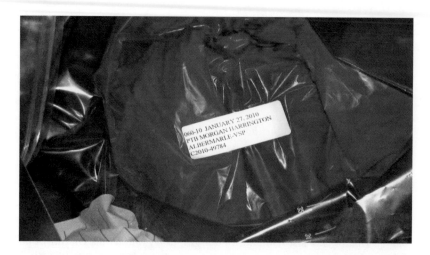

Some weeks after Morgan's funeral, I get a call from Allen Simpson. "We have a bag of Morgan's clothes here from the medical examiner's office. Frankly Gil, it's starting to smell. Do you want them? Or should we dispose of the bag?"

"Absolutely not. We want it. I'll come by and pick it up right away."

I drive down Peters Creek Road and pick up a big red hazmat bag from Simpsons' Funeral Home. Such a bizarre errand. I take the bag from Daniel. He used to play with Morgan at our house when he was a little boy.

Now I am taking this hideous putrid red bag from him. Unreal. The bag is squishy and sloggy and the stench of decay is overwhelming. I put the bag in the trunk of my car and drive away. The smell of rotten and death fills the car.

I can't stop crying.

I call Investigator Dino Cappuzzo immediately. Why do Morgan's clothes feel like a bag of soup and smell like Hell?

He assures me that all of Morgan's clothing is in evidence in Richmond, and every item is recorded and accounted for.

Then what's in the bag?

He's not sure.

We had planned to meet with Dino in Charlottesville the following day, and so will bring the red bag for him to check. I double-bag the red hazmat bag, which makes the smell somewhat more tolerable. It sits on the floor of the garage that night.

The next day, we step over the red bag repeatedly as we pack the car. Eventually, this strange burden is wedged in the back of Dan's car, next to Kirby's crate.

God, it smells.

We are relieved to turn the red bag over to Dino.

He calls later that day, chagrined, with a startling explanation.

In the red hazmat bag was all of Morgan's flesh and her hairmat, which was removed from her skeleton during autopsy. More obscenity. A talk about Morgan's hair should involve debate on the merits of highlights, or perhaps a new hairstyle, not a discussion of the hairmat that has been peeled away from her skull.

You can imagine--Morgan was killed October 17; it's now February--the stench.

We choose to see this abomination, this grotesque mistake--whose mistake is immaterial--in the best light. We resolve, deliberately, not to get hysterical and angry, but rather to be almost amused that Morgan found a way to take one last road trip with her family and sit next to her dog, as usual.

That's how Morgan becomes one of the very few people ever to have two cremations. The pouch of cremains from her second cremation is smaller, the ashes finer and rusty looking, the iron-red hue owing to the hemoglobin in her flesh.

This fine ruddy silt is as different from the earlier grey collection of ash Morgan's bones made, as night is from day.

Or as ashes are from our daughter.

Or as Morgan is from whoever slung her 115 pounds over his hulking shoulder that night, and climbed that steep, rounded Virginia mountain, crossing barbed wire fences and slipping on groundhog holes, to dump her limp, freshly dead body in that faraway drizzly dark pasture because he had completely finished with her.

Growth

It sounds contradictory. But the truth is, having a murdered daughter is easier than having a missing daughter. The wild pendulum swings between hope and despair for the 101 days Morgan was missing were excruciating to our family. Having recovered Morgan's body has provided some healing to us. The comfort gained from a funeral ritual is denied the families of the missing. There are no rituals for the missing. We are grateful to find more energy for forward motion after Morgan's funeral.

It is slow going, but we are figuring it out. We are determined to find the monster that murdered our Morgan. Stop him, and predators like him, from killing other girls.

I feel inadequate, poorly prepared, to take on a role of advocacy, and frankly we are pretty broken right now. At the most difficult time in our lives, we must continue to function at the very highest capacity we are capable of. We are determined to find justice for Morgan, and at the same time prevent predatory violence against other young women. Can we do it? Is it possible?

Loss is a resolute and determined teacher. Like the pounding surf, it can sculpt beautiful shapes, if you can tolerate the process, the destruction and reconfiguration. That mix of determination and acceptance is a choice, a difficult daily choice of accepting what is. Let go of what was. If you are particularly clever, at times there is joy to discover in what is unfolding here and now.

Morgan, you taught us so much. I believe that showing us how to grow strong enough to deal with your death is an infinitely precious final lesson. Morgan, your death gives us the opportunity to move into greater insight and greater love.

I get that; I really do, and believe it, though it ain't always easy to see. Every day has so many snares to pull me into negativity and self-pity. Walking Kirby, I see neighbors strapping grandbabies into car seats and wonder why that joy was never meant for us.

Here is where faith comes to the rescue, the belief that the direction of the universe is toward good and wholeness, despite all appearance of destruction. The pieces are falling into place, not apart. You cannot impose your desire on those pieces. They don't fit where you may want. Instead they will slip into the best, most appropriate place, of their own accord.

Mogo, we miss you terribly, constantly, and yet realize that you have made us grow. At the outer reaches of ability, you can fold, or hold determinedly to possibility and so discover character and hope.

Autopsy

Autopsy
Obscenity
How can this be
Scrounging in the fridge
For a little smidge
Maybe cheese?
And Bam! Forced to my knees
A glancing blow
From a photo
Mogo
On the do'
Oh no, here we go
Blindsided again
Coz every picture has a taint
And overlay clear, but faint
On each I see
Hologram of skull, rib, and phalange
Our baby
How can it be?

In reading the autopsy, we learned further brutal details about Morgan's murder, which included several rib fractures, a spiral-fractured left radius, and an incised fracture to the skull. Of particular note, her toxicology screens were negative.

February 24, 2010   *Closure*

People tell me that since Morgan's body has been found I can have closure. I don't think that is realistic or reasonable or even what I am looking for. This kind of abrupt fundamental loss is like having a traumatic severing of your arm. You don't get closure with an amputation. You are always aware of and wishing for your missing limb. BUT, you do have a choice-- to be crippled OR to learn to write with your non-dominant hand or with a prosthesis or stick a pen in your mouth and go for it. (Who knows, your penmanship may improve.) So you accommodate and learn to incorporate the injury into your reality. But the loss is ever present and apparent to self and others.

We don't know how to make this new life fabric yet. Often it looks like a tangled snarl that can never be sorted out--but sometimes I catch glimpses of something like a spider's web--delicate, intricate and having tremendous tensile strength. We are not there yet-- but see a direction to aim for.

241

—∞—

February 26, 2010   *Cigar Box*

Ashes in a cigar box. Morgan, we have your ashes setting on our coffee table. They are stored in one of you granddad's JGW cigar boxes. It seemed the right choice. We have several of them and use these boxes every day. Dad keeps change and keys and such on his dresser in a JGW cigar box. I store my tea and sweetener in a JGW cigar box on the kitchen counter and open it up every day. Alex has his filled with letters and photos. Predictably, you had used your JGW cigar box to store an assortment of funky jewelry.

Alex even found a photo of you as a baby, playing with jewelry in a JGW cigar box. Never could I have imagined a reality where you would be inside the box – waiting for the right day to be sprinkled outside and returned to the earth.

I was starting to spiral into the vortex of grief and loss, thinking, "we have only ashes left". How can we snatch meaning from Morgan's ashes-- but then I remembered that ashes can *be used to make cinder blocks which can be used to build strong foundations--for good--for education here at Virginia Tech Carilion School of Medicine and in Africa with OMNI School and who knows what else. We will pledge your ashes, mix and use your ashes as well as we can, to create some substantive good from this tragedy and in so doing honor the light that was Morgan Dana Harrington*

241

—∞—

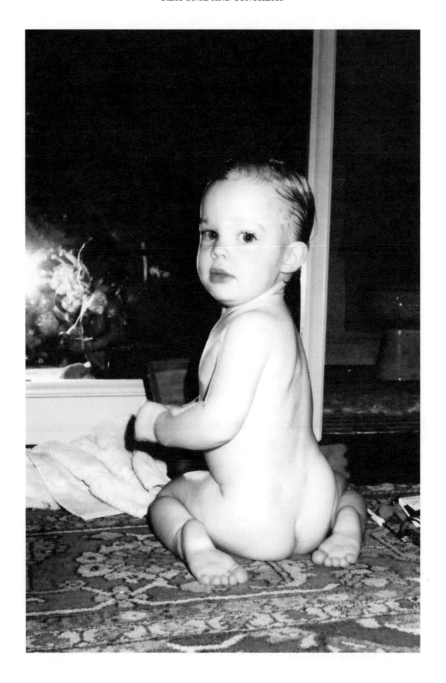

March 1, 2010   *Packing for Morgan*

I took some baby steps this week and started the breakdown of Morgan's apartment at Virginia Tech. It is a painful process to dismantle your child's life, especially when I recall all the joy and expectation we had when we moved her in only 18 months ago.

Morgan's apartment was great; comfortable, quirky and fun. She was the girl who had everything: a great apartment, friends, intelligence, and beauty. The only thing she had in limited supply was life—what a short life. What a tremendous waste.

Even thinking of that waste makes my breath choppy—I am only taking baby steps because it is so very difficult and also because I want to go slowly and savor the dismembering of the home Morgan had made. You can learn a lot about someone when you see the environment they create and how they live in it. It makes me happy and proud to see just how on top of things and how together Morgan's way of living was.

I take my time; enjoy these glimpses of the person she was becoming. Morgan was pretty special at the young age of 20. Given the chance to actually grow up, she was going to be absolutely phenomenal. Why couldn't it be?

241

—ɯɯ—

March 3, 2010   *Packing for OMNI*

Several of us from the Orphan Medical Network International medical mission team have started packing the 3,500 pounds of medical supplies we will take to Zambia, Africa, on our April medical trip. Anticipating the trip has me both excited and anxious. The separation from Dan is always painful, even more so this year because Morgan's death has left both of us vulnerable and raw. Despite the challenges that being apart will bring, I am more resolute than ever to make my journey to Africa. I was not able to save my precious child, but know that I will be able save other children's lives in Africa. Every bobble-headed baby with malaria we rehydrate and every burn we clean and dress negates some of the evil that is afloat in our world.

My pain will be less sharp, knowing I have made a practical and direct difference in our patients' and our students' chances for survival. This brings me much comfort. I keep trying to do my best to tip the scale in the direction of love. I do believe love is greater than hate and love will win in the end if we do our part to help it along.

241

---∿---

March 10, 2010   *Anxious*

We are so fragile, raw, more fear-based, which is not our typical state. We find ourselves locking up and checking things more at home. Dan still gets anxious if he calls me more than three times and I don't answer – afraid that I've been taken, too. Baseline, I am sloppy about the cell phone. I leave it in the car, or at home, or don't turn it on, or neglect to recharge it consistently. Seeing the fear in his eyes, I resolve to change my behavior.

Normally, I consider myself to be fairly strong and grounded. After Morgan was abducted and killed, I find I am not so sure of myself and easily overwhelmed. Regular stuff is more difficult. Even dropping the dog off at the vet is traumatic in a way. Ever since our girl didn't come back, all leave-takings are pain-filled.

Every single task I put my hand to reminds me of Morgan. I cook broccoli and start to reflexively put a portion aside for her. Morgan liked margarine, not butter like the rest of the family. These numerous meaningless incidentals in the course of my day invoke Morgan and pull me up short with a blast of grief and loss. It's like ripping the scab off a wound over and over and over. Will this ever heal?

241

March 15, 2010   *Husks*

I know we will be OK. That in no way diminishes the pain this murderer has inflicted on us, but rather is a testimonial to the closeness and love that we share. I see only three options and only one of them that I can embrace:

1.   *Crash and burn--won't let him kill us too.*
2.   *Paralysis-- won't let him damage us, nor compound the loss of Morgan's potential with the loss of our potential.*
3.   *Soldier on--continue to move forward, haltingly, even stumbling, even crawling--forward. Take what has been dealt us and be open-minded and creative and fashion new lives. This is undoubtedly the hardest task, but the only way I see some chance of salvation/reconciliation/peace.*

I believe this. I know it to be true, and STILL I feel the rage. Why? Many parallel emotions.

The anger is extinguished by the knowing – it is. The irrevocable primal knowing--the feel of the dry husks of your ribs. I cannot rage against such steadfast reality. To do so is wasted effort, foolish like raging against a mountain or a rock. It is what it is and will not change. Morgan is dead – Gil accept this truth.

241

—⚊⚊—

March 15, 2010   *Tat Attack*

Morgan, you are pulling us in your wake to places we've never imagined ourselves to be. Last week, you took Alex and me to a tattoo studio. Never thought I'd do this—but it seemed important to make some indelible manifestation on my body to commemorate the ending of your life. Your death is etched on my heart, my mind, my soul, but curiously, though a bit more haggard, my outside looked the same as when you were alive.

It's funny where people find meaning and comfort. I have no need of a gravestone or marker, but this personal, physical tribute is important to me this time. Alex and I were a little scared initially. (He made me go first.) The process was really pretty easy, minimal pain or fuss. We both got the 241 dots on our inner wrist, where we would catch sight of it throughout our day.

Morgan, your death has cut such a wide swathe through our lives that it seemed appropriate to have some physical sign of the impact on our bodies also. Alex and I are both happy with the symbols we now wear. It feels right, gives some kind of congruency that the outer is marked and changed as irrevocably as the inside has been. Dan is accepting, but made me promise that this would NOT be the beginning of a sleeve!

241

—✳—

March 17, 2010   *Night Vision*

The nights can be difficult. When you are between sleep and waking, your defenses dip and then unwanted thoughts and images come roaring in. I try not to think of how scared you were, the terror you felt. I try not to think of how much pain you were in as you were slaughtered.

Were you still alive when he brought you to Anchorage Farm? To be hunted like a deer running frantically over the hay stubble in the field, desperate to escape, trying to survive, crying, screaming, I see it. I hear it. Or, were you brought there already dead, like a slab of meat, carrion to be discarded and dumped in the field to rot. Just another carcass in the hunting preserve.

These images haunt me at night. During the day I can usually shake them off and focus on our job, trying to find your murderer. Other girls are in danger while this sadistic monster walks free. We will never rest until he is put away. Morgan, will you help us, in whatever way you can, to remove his evil from the world?

241

—✳—

March 19, 2010   *Savage*

I am leaving in two weeks on my medical mission to Africa and I find that I am reluctant to leave for the first time. I am reluctant to leave because there is still evil afoot in this town, and I think foolishly that if I am here, in some way I can stop HIM, and he must be stopped. There is a man/monster in Charlottesville, Virginia, who likes to hunt and kill young girls like prey, and who makes sport out of killing.

Most hunters have the integrity to kill in a humane and quick fashion. This man doesn't work like that. He enjoys the hunting part of a kill and chooses to kill in a savage and brutal way. This Charlottesville man hurt Morgan Harrington enough to break her bones before he murdered her. I cannot get the image of Morgan's shattered bones out of my mind, nor the jagged feel of the fractures from my fingers—a violent, sadistic, and dangerous man.

As a mother, I beg the young women of this town to be prudent, and to look after each other. I ask the community to be a community, be involved and be vigilant, and find this monster in your midst and protect your young. He must be found. This is not his first crime and he has upped his game in a significant and disturbing way.

241

March 22, 2010 *Springless*

The basic assumptions we held about our life are wrong now and must be remade and adjusted. Like, we have no daughter anymore. It is painful and hard to reconfigure our reality. I have to watch myself and not let that pain turn me bitter and sour. I started to go that way working in the yard the other day cleaning up some of the debris and twigs from a very long winter.

Usually this task is fun for me. I enjoy seeing the greening of the earth and feeling the burgeoning life that spring brings forth. This year I didn't allow that quickening of joy in myself. Instead my internal dialogue was, "the very dirt is coming alive today, but that box of ashes on the coffee table is as dead and inert as it was a week ago, and as dead as it'll be a year from now. It isn't right." Not a good direction for my thoughts. The pitfalls and pity parties are everywhere.

Our new life is devoid of much joy--perhaps we will find it sometime in the future. We are still working on survival. The caring and love of others pulls me from despair the path to survival. Once we have mastered survival we can encourage the blossoming of joy again. Some day.

241

March 24, 2010 *Tilled*

I strive to be open-minded enough to allow and recognize the good that is trying to unfold from Morgan's death. My tendency is always to try to enhance, take remnants and craft something new. The minefield of memories and emotions we now live with makes it difficult to maintain a positive, forward-moving *attitude. It is vital to me, Morgan, that your existence not be wasted. I will not allow your essence to drain away. Somehow we will find a way to use the water of your life to nourish seeds and create growth.*

I recognize that seeds sprout and grow best on clear and open soil. Our old lives have been plowed under and we have been tilled, ripped open. Can we be wise to accept and germinate new seeds? I believe we can. We will be creative and diligent and clever enough to allow growth to occur. I promise you this, Morgan.

We will do the work you were not allowed to finish; we will feed and teach children, educate young people and keep girls safe – for you in your name, so that you were here matters to the world and your being taken from us has impact and meaning in your community at large.

No "fade to close" for your young life – your essence and your motivation must continue to flourish and you will NOT be forgotten!

241

—⟶—

March 26, 2010   *Take Back the Night*

Thursday, Dan and I traveled to Blacksburg to speak at the Virginia Tech Take Back the Night rally. This message of safety for women and children has always been important to us, but now in the face of Morgan's murder it is pivotal to our belief structure. Somehow, we have tacitly given acceptance that it's okay in America for men to prey upon half the population. Our exaggerated culture of self has reintroduced a primitive Darwinian way of life—survival of the fittest, each one for himself. Most civilized societies pride themselves on their level of integration and complexity of connections, NOT how an individual can place his own needs and urges paramount.

I am not a theorist to critique and dissect how this perversion has come to pass, only know it must stop and no longer be tolerated. Part of the change process is awareness and repudiation of social mores that encourage the continued violence and predation against women. The Take Back the Night rally focuses attention on the problem and encourages change to occur.

Morgan Harrington should have been safe in the John Paul Jones Arena parking lot. She was NOT asking for it. She was NOT provocatively dressed, no cleavage and nothing tight. In fact, as I stress time and again, the only skin she had hanging out was her beautiful face. Can men learn not to vanquish women as disposable objects? I believe that they can and must. A campaign to limit violence is really basic, the lowest common denominator. Our mandate should be respect, and cherish. But denouncing predatory behavior and gender violence is a beginning, so let's start here.

241

—∞—

March 30, 2010   *Like a Child Leaps*

At times I am angry but never so angry to forget how much love we have shared and the joy we had as a family. My heart will hold fast to that love until despair is turned away.

Love and goodness define what a lifetime is all about. People turn toward love like plants turn toward light and are renewed. It is important to reinforce this positive outlook tonight as negative factors gather in the periphery of our lives to feed like vultures upon the event of your demise, Morgan. That mindset is so foreign to me that I really cannot comprehend it. It is probably a mistake to waste any time analyzing evil anyway—detracts from our goal of forward positive motion.

We are making it and finding a way forward despite many challenges. I really have been mired down by what your death involved—why such a terribly brutal ending for my sweet girl? But it was an ending—not THE END. Your being will still have meaning and impact through the good works we do in your name. The suffering, I manage by recalling the quotation, "The soul leaves the body quickly and with joy—like a child leaps from the schoolyard gate."

Leap and fly high, my little one, dragon-dancer. We are OK alone here.

241

—∞—

Mom,

I love you so much & hope you have a wonderful mother's day. You & dad have been such a great support system for me this year & I really appreciate all you've done for me (& Amy). It was hard not having you there to talk to & smooch. while you were in Zambia but I know you do wonderful work there. I'm so proud of you.

Love mokie. .::.

♡ 2410k ♡ 2009

April 1, 2010   *Westboro*

Dear Friends,

I am in the starting blocks for departure to Africa to care for the impoverished people in the deep bush of Zambia. It is always difficult to leave my home and family, but I know that this work is mine to do.

I regret that turmoil and controversy are threatening my family and our community during my absence. I know you are strong enough and I know Dan is strong enough to meet this challenge to our core value of goodness and positive forward motion.

Strength is developed by caring heavy weights. This is just one more to shoulder and use to enhance our collective muscle mass.

If, (God willing) we have electricity, I will continue to blog from Zambia whenever possible to update you on our clinic work and the groundbreaking of the Morgan Harrington Educational Wing at OMNI Village, Ndola, Zambia, the school we are building to honor Morgan's life and her desire to participate in OMNI's work.

Thank all or you for holding us up. The journey continues to be difficult, but our path is secure with so many pointing the way. We send our love to Blacksburg and to Virginia Tech with these two messages:

To the Blacksburg Community:

As you may know, the Westboro Baptist Church, which we do not consider a church at all, but a group of domestic terrorists, has chosen to target our murdered daughter Morgan Harrington with a hate rally in Blacksburg on 4/9/10. Yes, there is evil in the world and this latest strike from it is painful and disturbing, but nothing compared to the death blow we have just survived. I don't understand how this evil gathering, which clearly appears to be a political entity, can cloak themselves in religiosity and thereby gain constitutional protection and financial indemnity.

I am not courageous enough to be one who seeks out all the evil in the world to vanquish it, but I am not cowardly enough to turn my back on it and run either. When evil like the WBC presents you must face it and keep your eye on it as you attempt to neutralize its poison.

We will not let this petty evil topple us. We will shine the light and dispel the darkness of intimidation and domestic terrorism. We will continue to work for good, as caregivers, as educators, as advocates, feeding the poor, washing their feet, and binding their wounds. We will not be diverted from these tasks we have taken on in Morgan's honor. We will not allow Morgan's killer to erase her from the world nor these petty thugs to poison her legacy.

Darkness must always give way to the light. We will prevail.

Gil and Dan Harrington

To Virginia Tech's Hokie Nation:

I feel your sorrow as you brace for another blast of evil on Blacksburg – the Westboro Baptist group's planned hate rally on April 9, 2010.

Please do not respond in kind to these domestic terrorists. Instead, be strong and let your heart lights shine – hold a concurrent silent candle light vigil in support of the Virginia Tech community as a whole and Morgan Harrington, in particular.

Protest passively to protect one of your own – your Hokie sister, Morgan Harrington, from this post mortem assault. Stop evil in its tracks. Zero tolerance for hatred!

Be safe, be silent, be dignified, no arrests (of Hokies) but passively resist the evil that has come to town. Eradicate the darkness and hate of the WBC with your light.

241

Gil and Dan Harrington

———

April 12, 2010 *Posted by Dan*

Gil Harrington's thoughts from April 12th, 2010

Gil has been in Zambia since April 5, 2010. She and the OMNI team have been busy with setting up and then taking down their clinic operation in the Zambian bush. Gil was hoping to be able to continue to blog but Zambia is a third world country with poverty, little water, little food, and limited electricity. The lack of modern technology makes blog transmission near impossible.

Gil has called me three times since arriving in Zambia and each phone conversation lasts about 60 seconds. She has been able to get lost in her work and have a bit of insulation from the protest and the stress of having a murdered daughter.

Gil wanted me to post her experience in the bush from this past Friday. During the OMNI clinic, a young mother came with her sick female child, asking for help. The child was very ill with fever and dehydration from malaria. Malaria is endemic to Zambia and is one of the major killers in the population.

95

Quickly, the severity of the child's illness was recognized and Gil was asked to take the mother and child to a distant hospital on the only transportation available, a local bus.

The trip was complicated by the fact that the mother did not speak English and Gil did not speak Bemba, the local language, but fortunately the bus driver spoke a little French and Gil was able to communicate with him by speaking French. During the trip, the child became more ill and stopped breathing. Gil was screaming in French for the driver to hurry, hurry! Gil revived the child and ultimately they arrived at the hospital with the child still clinging to life. The child died the next day.

Gil, crying as she tells me this story, said her trip to Zambia was a way to save other children when she could not save Morgan; but she found that she couldn't save this little girl. Gil sees the fragility of life in every face she sees and all the work she does.

241

———∞———

April 26, 2010   *From Zambia*

The OMNI medical team trip to Zambia was intense and transformative as it always is. We work so hard. Our team of 16 saw close to 4000 patients in 11 days! We see so many and so much that it is disorienting. Then we get on a plane for a 26+ hour journey back to the USA and try to make sense of it all.

After arriving in Ndola, Zambia we went directly from the airport to the OMNI Village site. The 156 students at the school had been waiting for hours in the red dust and sun to welcome us. The kids line up, oldest to youngest, boys and girls separately, all so proudly wearing their school uniforms. They welcome us singing and chanting in Bemba and English. A particularly moving line in a song is, "OMNI feeds us so we may live and show what love is about". And we do. The one full meal per day, for some, the only nourishment they receive, which OMNI furnishes for our 156 students, is fundamental to their health and growth, creating a zone of safety for them that allows for focus and learning to occur. These kids are being educated to help them break out of a bare subsistence existence and become leaders in their community and their country.

The groundbreaking for the Morgan Harrington Educational Wing has started. This facility will allow us to add grades 7, 8, and 9 to our program. I am thrilled to have Morgan be a fundamental part of educating young people in Zambia. Morgan planned to travel with me to Zambia to see the OMNI School and the children she had heard so much about. Her murder ended those plans, BUT her work and her dream of educating children will continue.

Morgan will make a difference in so many young lives. She is gone but her legacy lives on in a beautiful and magnificent way.

241

April 28, 2010

The medical clinics are controlled chaos. So many folks come out for the only western medical care many will receive in a year. Our OMNI clinics served 500+ patients per day. We provide physicians, a full pharmacy, lab testing, and wound care. When possible, we distribute rice/salt/beans during the clinics. This food distribution requires armed guards as crowd control because there is such desperation and need.

There is such a kaleidoscope of colors and faces, (and for me in wound care, legs and feet), screaming babies, noise, flies, dust, and heat. The team gels quickly and becomes focused and determined to do as much as we possibly can to help these impoverished and deserving people.

Some villages are doing better than others. You look out at the triage line of about 600 people and note that half of them have shoes. That's a good sign. You note that the kids' hair is mostly dark, not red from protein depletion or patchy with scabies infestation, another good sign. Then there are communities where almost no one has shoes, the kids are dressed in clothing tattered into ribbons, and their protruding, hard bellies are full of worms, not food.

The rains were just ending so malaria is on the upswing. Bobble-headed, glassy-eyed babies are limp in the arms of grandmothers. These elders now are primary caregivers because of a missing parental generation, ravaged by malaria and HIV/AIDS. So many wasted faces, young and old alike, with sunken temples and cheekbones like knife blades.

Suffering can serve as a catalyst for compassion. Suffering can open my understanding of possibility. Renovation follows demolition. I remind myself of these truths constantly, and still, I have weak moments.

One afternoon I was feeling particularly sorry for myself. It seemed that everyone else's life was punctuated with fun events, birthdays, weddings, celebrations, and all I had was the box of Morgan's ashes on the coffee table in the living room. No fun, no future.

I gave myself a stern talking to and asked for guidance. I slowly realized that even here was opportunity.

Ashes are cinders. Which can be used to make cinderblock.

Even from this difficult spot, we can synthesize, we can build. I took a pocket full of Morgan's ashes/cinders with me to Zambia and mixed them into the foundation of what would become the Morgan Harrington Educational Wing at OMNI Village. Hundreds of children will be educated in that building and given the tools necessary for productive, successful lives, and the prospect of safer, healthier children of their own.

Construction went remarkably fast, considering that bricks were made on site, hand-cut from the ubiquitous hardened termite mounds that rise everywhere in the surrounding scrubby mango fields, with mortar and cement mixed in barrels, and all labor, carrying, lifting, everything, done by hand. The Morgan Harrington Educational Wing was completed and dedicated in December, 2012. Dr. Maureen Mwanawasa, revered in Zambia as its cultured, eloquent former First Lady, officiated at the opening. Drums pounded, women trilled and sang, and all the village danced.

That joy, in this case a grateful community celebrating its children's and grandchildren's better futures, new friends, even a better understanding between two cultures, is how you triumph over evil. You transmute what remains into something good.

With that belief, I remind myself, you can do great and lasting things, even when you start with just a handful of ashes.

241

—⟶⟵—

April 30, 2010

A few days after arriving in Zambia, the OMNI team held a clinic at Kasango, a rural community half an hour from Ndola. Wound care is my station, but during a rare lull in my usual long line of patients, I was asked to accompany a little 10-month baby girl, Gift Pasella, to the hospital. Our pediatrician had examined Gift and found her significantly dehydrated and febrile and wanted the child admitted for IV hydration and malaria treatment. We gave a dose of Panadol for fever and I got on the bus with Gift and family. This is the story I tried to tell Dan hurriedly over a tenuous phone connection.

Ten minutes into the ride the baby grew more lethargic and stopped whimpering. Her breathing became frighteningly erratic.

Our driver is tearing over the unpaved road as fast as he can. I'm urging him to go faster as I watch terror spread over the Mama's face and watch the baby's tiny fingers turn from a flat dusky brown to white as pearls. Several times, she stopped breathing altogether. I was unwrapping her from the mother's sling and pouring water over her to cool her down, praying, "Please, please, not this little one too. Oh God, why?"

We did get to the hospital. The baby died shortly thereafter.

I am still working on how to process this loss. The baby's death does give me some perspective though. I have felt cheated to have had Morgan for only 20 years. I doubt that Gift's Mama was even 20 and she had her child for only 10 months. A dramatic reminder that life of whatever duration should be celebrated exactly as this baby was named, a gift.

241

—⟶⟵—

OMNI Reverie

Squatting in the dust
the pose I must
take
to make
my way through, this dark forest.
The wounds I tend,
skin I try to mend,
on all the limbs
of hers and hims.
Catching only glimpses of the faces.
my task's in other places.
It's the feet I know so well.
The stories the toes can tell.
Ceaseless work since he was born
turned this farmer's soles to horn.
Scrawny, birdlike children's feet,
so spare of flesh,
so little to eat.
The blazing joy
in this boy
as I put
his bandaged foot
in its first shoe.
Who knew
the good we could do?
Soak and clean
coating legs with Vaseline
under African sun.
My kind of fun.
The heart sings.
What pleasure service brings.
Axe wounds and ulcers,
scrapes and burns obscene,
these are the feet I tend and clean.
And with each wound I bind,

I find,
and do amaze,
that healing flows both ways.

241

G.M. Harrington

May 3, 2010   *Reproach*

Returning from the other side of the world is always difficult. You are tired and jet-lagged, and regardless try to jump right back into a full schedule. I was prepared for that challenge. What I was not prepared for was being back at square one with my grief for Morgan. It was like her murder had just happened, the rawness and the pain, shocking in intensity.

Before I left for Zambia, I had managed to find a place of some peace and equilibrium, fragile though it was. Suddenly, I was overwhelmed, bombarded by the obscenity of our loss anew. How could someone have brutally murdered our shiny wonderful girl? How could this have happened to her? To us?

I felt besieged, attacked. Even small things grated. Photos of Morgan that I had previously found refuge in, her sweet face all around our house, now a reproach, not comfort. "Why me? You didn't keep me safe. He walks free and I am only dust, in your hands." The unfairness and the waste of her great promise just infuriates.

I guess I need some time, time to make all the bargains and adjustments necessary to cushion this mortal blow to our family--again. Time to relinquish all the dreams and plans, the assumptions about a future--again.

I am tired. It is tempting to give up, but I am not so flat busted that I can allow his evil to go unchecked. I will dig deep. I can find tomorrow at least, sure of that much.

241, My little Mogo.

—〰—

May 5, 2010   *How many shirts*

My reserves are further stressed this week by closing out Morgan's apartment in Blacksburg. Mine to do, I know. Both an honor, and a most taxing obligation. I really liked the chance to have my hands in the mix of her life one last time. To read all Morgan's scrawled lists and post- its everywhere. She was so busy, so many plans to do and accomplish. Smell her t-shirts. Shake my head over impossibly high-heeled shoes and tattered, ratty sneakers.

We had moved her into that apartment such a short time ago, with such hopes and plans for her future. Morgan had such a wonderful, rich, together life. Just devastating that someone could end it all, end her very life with his hate and depravity.

As I sift and sort Morgan's things, some of my inner dialogue is ridiculous, even to me. I'm trying to figure out what to keep and what to discard. All feels precious because it has an association to Morgan, but it is overwhelming and not practical to keep it all. So I find myself asking, how many shirts does a dead girl need in her closet? What's the rule of thumb/protocol for this aberrant reality we live in?

I realize there's no rule. The gauge is me. How much is enough so that when I open her closet or drawer I can get a sense of her, but not so many empty things and NO Morgan that I am undone. It's a delicate compromise to find just where the zone of comfort is for us, where memory cues remind us of our precious daughter, but not so intensely that we are engulfed and drown in the loss once more.

241

May 6, 2010   *Supplicant*

My heart is so heavy. I am overwhelmed by the violence and negativity. What is happening to our world? In 2010 we really should be working to establish respect and cherish between all people. And yet we are stuck, still battling for basic safety--please don't hurt me, again.

The reign of indifference and the culture of complacency that provides the breeding ground for this festering violence is a formidable obstacle to change. Not sure I have it in me to stand against such an entrenched and strong status quo. Thought I only had to take on Morgan's killer, not the system that created him.

I pray for strength. I pray for direction. Not proud of those please, please prayers, but please.

Mogo.

241

May 18, 2010   *A Letter from the Dead*

I had a phone call four months after Morgan's remains were discovered. The caller introduced herself, "My name is Jane Vance. You don't know me, but I have something of Morgan's that I need to bring to you. I am traveling out of the country in a few days, and I want you to have this before I go."

I knew exactly who Jane was, Morgan's beloved teacher from Virginia Tech. We met the next day.

Jane brought an extraordinary gift. The last class assignment Jane gave her students asked them to write about the person who has had the most significant impact in the student's life. This assignment required the students to be creative, architects, to imagine and illustrate a shrine dedicated to those who have inspired and shaped their lives.

In the writing component of the assignment, a student explains what gifts and insights the teacher gave the student. Finally, Jane asked them to reflect: "Because of your teacher, who do you promise to become?" Morgan left her essay with Jane after completing the assignment, with the instructions: please give this essay to my mother someday.

Jane explained that Morgan had stayed after class and come up to her lectern immediately after hearing the assignment, excited to ask if she could bend the directions a bit and choose two teachers, since she wanted to dedicate her shrine to both her mama and her papa. Jane said yes.

Imagine the emotion and elation of receiving such a gift after your daughter has been murdered. Morgan's shrine essay is incredibly intimate and beautiful, one of our greatest treasures.

241

—⚬—

Morgan Harrington
The Creative Process
Spring, 2009
Ms. Vance

My Place

I actually struggled with this assignment because I really wanted to include meaningful, not just pretty objects in my shrine. When you really pare down the pile, removing all the pretty leaves and shells, there are very few items that hold profound value. After some thought, I was able to create what I imagine would be a lovely shrine, based in the woods behind my deceased grandparents' home in Charlottesville, Virginia.

I chose the location to be in my grandparents' forest because when I reminisce about my childhood, I almost always picture myself crouched down on a flattened boulder in the middle of the lazy creek, fishing for crawdaddies with my tiny hands. My Poppi's ashes were scattered in that creek, along with several other loved ones'. Although my maternal grandparents were not always happy people, they were always interesting individuals, and they helped shape who I am because they raised the most important person in my life, my mother. An imagined lock of her strawberry blonde hair is nestled into the deep center of my pile-shaped shrine as the relic because I love her so much and strive to be more like her.

One of the central objects in my shrine is a huge comfy chair that my Dad sits in every night to finish his work from the office. All throughout my youth, I would jump up on his lap to share this chair, and nudge his pile of never-ending work aside with my grass-stained toes. He would never shove me off and continue to work, as some adults might have done. Instead, he always took the few extra minutes to cuddle and show that he loved me, despite all of his expectations at work.

In my shrine, I include items to define who I am. At the base of my shrine, there is a long expanse of snake skin that has peeled off a snake's back, bit by bit. To me, this sloughing symbolizes the learning and growth that I have achieved in my 19 years, and it reminds me of the changes that I need to continue to make in order to develop into an adult. Crowded around the shrine, piled in stacks, spilling out onto the earth, are dozens of fiction novels. I am an avid reader and have always indulged this love, maybe more than I should. The presence of the books shows their importance to me and reminds me that social relationships can be more dangerous than fictional ones; however, they are more generous, as well. With reminders of complexity and insight, I will prosper.

Finally, I balanced an incense burner near the bottom of the shrine to symbolize spirituality. I look to my mom as a spiritual example because she is so open-minded. She is a very spiritual person and I see how this trust enriches her life, so I plan to spend more time exploring higher powers and positive energies instead of focusing on things that are insignificant in comparison.

Overall, my shrine is composed with reminders. It is easy to get in a monotonous routine and forget about the real work and explorations I intend to accomplish and enjoy in my life. Thinking of the meaning of my shrine, I have a higher likelihood of succeeding in transforming into the completely grown-up Morgan, so thank you for the assignment.

—∞—

May 10, 2010   *Mother's Day*

I was the recipient of much extra love and support yesterday on Mother's Day. Folks anticipated that I might have a tough time as I relinquished my role as mother to Morgan. But, I haven't done so yet--and the day was really fine.

Mothering has always involved caring for, not just caring about my kids. The multitude of tasks I do for my family are manifestations of love and caring and I have enjoyed them as such. Brushing out tangles from Morgan's long hair, packing lunches, hot banana bread, filling up her gas tank, mountains of laundry, these Mother's chores are a daily, tangible, and practical demonstration of my love.

I cannot surrender my role as mom to Morgan just yet. That day will come and I know I will mourn the closing of that part of my life. But right now my job of parenting and protecting is not done, Morgan is asking for, demanding the biggest task ever: find her murderer. I still have work to do for my little girl.

As long as this last obligation remains, I hold fiercely to my role as Morgan's mom. When she has justice I will concede to being mother of one, but not one minute before.

241
Mogo

—∞—

May 12, 2010   *Traditions*

I am disturbed by the reign of indifference and the culture of complacency about violence on campuses, particularly at UVA. Yeardley Love's murder in Charlottesville is being attributed to a breakdown in communication. That is simply blame shifting. Instead, what seems to have occurred, again, is a breakdown in imparting and enforcing expectations, as if there is a policy of acceptance within the system, enabling violence and assaults to continue to occur unchecked.

Over the years many students' lives have been devastated by predatory acts on campus. It's a new day and our world is experiencing an escalation of violence everywhere--and on campuses now, lives are being lost, not just disrupted. The body count is rising. When will that number be significant enough to provoke real, substantive, thoughtful introspection and accountability, not just platitudes that support the status quo?

It is a new day. It is a time for a different response. Ugly, tragic, violent things have happened in your community to precious young lives, on your watch. It is time to do the honorable thing and NOT turn aside.

241

—⁂—

May 14, 2010   Reluctant

The official response to violence on campus is kind of like the response of some authorities to 9/11. They were directing folks back into the buildings, unable to even conceive of a world where such an atrocity could occur, acts of violence bigger and more lethal than had been seen before.

The world has changed.

Another incident changed our assumptions about violence in schools, Columbine. The world has changed.

There has been a cluster phenomenon of hideous violence in Virginia, at both universities, Virginia Tech and University of Virginia. The world has changed. You have been placed in a position where you can be prime movers on the forefront of devising an effective response strategy, or you can keep directing your students back into the burning building. Business as usual and squander more lives as well as an opportunity for greatness.

Virginians are reluctant to give up traditions, but the tradition and culture that tolerates violence in your midst must be addressed.

The world has changed.

241

—⁂—

May 17, 2010   Smug

It has been seven months since Morgan was abducted, raped, and murdered. Still no resolution! We find some comfort in having recovered her body; knowing is better than not knowing and trying to "fill in the blanks".

We are getting more frantic. Not for answers, we have our answer – Morgan is dead. The incidentals of how he did it, or why he did it, don't really

matter. What DOES matter is that he is still out there. This wasn't his first assault against a woman. He worked up to the crime of murder--but he is there now! Somewhere in the back of his mind he is figuring out another dump site – like Anchorage farm – just in case. So when the next opportunity presents itself, he is ready.

I feel him. He is smug, he got away with it – again. Secrets don't keep forever. So far the only breaks we have gotten are Morgan's bones - but the truth will out, in its own time, and our time is coming, it just has to be. If he is lucky, he will only be doing time.

Charlottesville, cough up this predator. Those who know need to speak before he acts again.

241

—⚶—

May 19, 2010   *White Ribbons*

Maybe institutions are starting to get it, to be able to listen to the clamor of voices that ask for and demand acknowledgement and justice for the crimes against them.

I love the "white ribbon campaign against violence"-- visible symbols to be distributed at graduation at UVA this week. There must be more attention given to violence on campus, and 25 thousand white ribbons is an awful lot of stuff to sweep under the rug.

Kent State, four dead, changed the direction of the nation. In Virginia, half a dozen young people missing, and--nothing. How can this be? Here in Virginia we have literally had a child's severed head handed over to police in a coffee shop, and we do--nothing?

One factor sociologists use to evaluate the development of a culture is to assess how that group cares for its women and children. Your statistics on this don't look good. Parents send their precious children to college to gain skills for life, not to have their lives snatched away.

A prestigious degree is nice, but do we as parents need to factor into the cost of that prestigious degree whether our kid will make it out alive?

241

—⚶—

Test Results from Morgan's Shirt

A core group of relentless supporters has coalesced around our family, determined to find justice for Morgan and help save the next girl. Together, we advocate for safety, and solicit information that will lead to an arrest in Morgan's unsolved homicide case. We host press conferences, vigils, balloon releases, and numerous other events to raise awareness.

On May 11, 2010, Dino Cappuzzo and Ed McDowell from VSP meet at our home in Roanoke with information about a new development. Morgan's shirt, which had been found in November, 2009, on 15th Street in Charlottesville, has yielded DNA that matches a 2005 abduction/rape/attempted murder case in Fairfax, Virginia, with an unknown perpetrator.

We feel more hopeful. We still don't know who killed Morgan, but when we find him, we will know he is the murderer. We will get this guy.

I find myself asking, was the DNA from hair or semen? Does it matter? My thought processes have become so warped. I actually experience some elation when I hear that the DNA was derived from a bloodstain of the murderer on Morgan's shirt. I know you fought like crazy, Morgan.

Good girl. You had so much to live for.

Law enforcement brought a composite sketch that the Fairfax victim had created with a forensic artist. For the first time, we look into the face of evil.

The one who killed our daughter. We call him Sketch.

DATE/TIME: 9/24/05 (Saturday)10:00 P.M

LOCATION: Oxford Row Townhouses
(Rock Garden Drive)
(Park/Swimming pool area)

SYNOPSIS:
Female victim (26 YOA) was walking home from the Giant Food store located on Jermantown Rd. The suspect grabbed the victim from behind as she was walking down Rock Garden Drive. The suspect carried the victim to the park/pool area where he sexually assaulted her. The suspect was last seen running south behind the pool towards Fairhaven Court.

The Sketch image is broadcast widely in Charlottesville and beyond. Help Save the Next Girl's advocate Amanda St.Clair posts the Sketch image in just about every gas station and restaurant in Albemarle County.

Our Help Save the Next Girl champions are so determined to capture Sketch that they even put his ugly visage on car magnets which they affix to their vehicles. I try, but cannot have the magnet on my car. It puts me off my game as I leave the grocery store and see his face. I just cannot do it.

—⚬—

May 21, 2010   *Flat*

As a family we are taking on water. Valiantly trying, but sinking nonetheless because we have lost the joy of being.

We have the work component down in spades. We do the work to sustain each other, the work to fulfill our roles in the community, the work of our jobs. We are prodigious taskers. The work gives us direction.

But seven months in, we are all coming up against--why bother? What does it matter?

I know a steady diet of only work won't sustain us. We need a reason to keep moving forward. The joy of living, but we don't really feel OK with joy right now. Kind of like we think feeling joy is selling out on Morgan. Know that if we don't find it we will sell out on life itself.

Dan and I have always had an undercurrent of lightness and fun between us. We revel in our relationship. But this is such a hard, hard place. We need that little circuit of joy, however we can't see past our poor dead Morgan. The empty room, the neatened closet, all flat. Even her car has died. (Need to call for a jump.) We all need a jump-start--Morgan's car, Dan, Alex, and I—to get some energy flowing so we can start moving forward again.

241

—⚬—

May 26, 2010   *Afraid*

We returned yesterday from out of town. It was difficult to leave the refuge of our home for several days. Being away seemed to open vulnerabilities in me. Just didn't manage to compose myself and protect myself in the usual way, perhaps because I had less control, less predictability, or just didn't know how to read the cues in a different environment.

I found myself ambushed by anguish and tears at unexpected moments: at dinner, in an elevator, even at the airport. I am surprised to be falling apart in this way so many months after Morgan's murder. Shouldn't it be getting better?

Ironically it was also hard to return home to Roanoke. Our sense of sanctuary here has been shattered. I guess we will never feel totally safe again anywhere. That's one of the ways we have been changed by our encounter with evil.

That violation makes us feel more fragile and act more cautiously. I check the doors and windows more often now. I rarely open them to catch the morning breeze and I draw the blinds early against the night's blackness. I wonder if this will improve after the arrest of Morgan's killer. I hope so; I don't want to contemplate the rest of our lives colored with fear.

241

—⟋⟍—

June 2, 2010   *Calling Cards*

Our beautiful shiny original, out of the box girl, is now firmly in the box, on our coffee table. Our time together has ended, an ending, but not THE END. Now we have to figure out how to proceed, to move forward in a positive way. It's tricky to keep yourself open enough to recognize and allow goodness to unfold.

I had a nice burst of joy this weekend when I recognized some calling cards from Morgan. Alex and I spent a long, unsuccessful day apartment hunting for him. As we entered the last place on the list I noticed a string of tattered Tibetan prayer flags flapping on a fence nearby, but the apartment was just dreadful. We walked away and had a conversation about how we both were waiting for a "communication or a calling card" from Morgan. Maybe the prayer flags (which Morgan loved and hung in her space at home and at Virginia Tech) meant nothing.

We walked on and watched two small children playing on the sidewalk ahead of us, laughing and squealing in the sun. As we got closer we saw that their excitement centered on a small contraption at the curb that was cranking out clouds of bubbles. A bubble machine! The only other bubble machine I have ever seen was at Morgan's funeral/celebration.

We proceeded down the block and a man came right out of a realty office carrying a sign: Apartments, Apartments, Apartments. We stopped. The agent took us directly to a phenomenal place and we made the deposit.

In a span of 15 minutes- prayer flags, bubble machine, rental. I get it. Thank you, Morgan.

241

—∞—

June 4, 2010   *Kudzu*

We don't cry for the dead. We cry for ourselves, our pain, our loss, our grief. Seems like a self-indulgent activity, one that leaves us drained and spent. So stop it. Why cry? Instead we should cling to routine and pretense, praying that it will hold us until gaps open in this wall of pain.

I am hoping that eventually tiny root hairs of normal will sprout and anchor.

With luck, normalcy will grow enough to crack the immense wall of hurt. I know that solid wall will never erode into nothingness, but I'm going to try so hard to grow all over that pain. Germinate and smother it like kudzu, obliterating its shape and form with a dense, verdant curtain. Maybe then we'll feel alright.

241

—∞—

June 7, 2010   *Scars*

Sorrow is an untamed dog, at times fawning and at others fierce. Sorrow has sharp teeth. It likes to take up your arm with a soft mouth and then lay the pinpoints of its bite on your skin. Barely piercing the membrane, hardly hurts at all, just to remind you that it's there and that sorrow knows no master. Other times sorrow chews and gnaws, relentlessly abrading away protective tissue. On occasion, and more often than I like, sorrow erupts like a savage beast and rips and tears at the flesh of our composure.

We bear the scars of many such encounters with sorrow and grief. I choose to see these scars as beautiful, evidence of our survival and perseverance. A scar represents the body's phenomenal ability to heal after wounds and if you grow one it is a badge of honor and you are one of the lucky ones who have survived and transcended injury.

Morgan suffered mortal blows. No scars there. We are hurting and healing and will never rest until justice prevails and this Charlottesville killer with his brutal fists is taken off the streets.

Survival is good. A start. Will joy ever emerge again?

241

—〰—

June 11, 2010   *Don't resist*

Suffering is a call to change pain into wisdom and compassion, an opportunity for transformation and growth. I get that, but understanding it and living it are two different propositions.

I see the way. I have to let go of my stuff, my plans, and surrender. Just give it over and let the hours and the years be what they will. Accept the life we have been given and find the goodness in it. I know this surrender is the only way to survive the tragedy of Morgan's death. I think I am actually doing it at times, but the mind is tricky.

Without my even realizing it, resistance and backward thinking start to creep into my head. Internally I replay all the what ifs, why us, it's so unfair, and in an instant I am right back at square one in a puddle of self-pity—it's indulgent and not helpful.

As a nurse, when I give an injection, I try to position the arm so the muscle is relaxed. I explain to the patient not to tense the muscle as I enter the skin to minimize pain at the injection site.

This is the key; to soften to the piercing of pain. Don't resist. Accept the pain. If you can, even embrace the pain, engulf it, and allow it to pass through you. Use it. Be opened by it, more connected and more compassionate to our shared vulnerabilities and weakness.

This is a hard lesson, but I'm motivated by knowing that the fellow who doesn't listen and really tenses up his arm during an injection often ends up having to get stuck again.

241

—〰—

June 16, 2010 *Father's Day, AND--from Alex*

So because Morgan is unable to wish you a Happy Father's Day I will do it for both of us. I know this had been the hardest year of our lives. We have all been dealt a blow that will forever change who we are and our family dynamic. Throughout this entire experience, you have been the rock upon which we have all built some sense of normalcy.

You have been husband, protector, banker, sounding board, computer whiz, media commentator, lobbyist, doctor, and friend. Look at all the hats you have been forced to wear that are all an extension of FATHER. You have allowed yourself to feel the grief of Morgan's loss and shown Mom and me that it is okay to let down your guard and feel this immeasurable pain. You have been a model that in spite of or perhaps because of this aching, we all feel you can still face the world and work even harder, and do so with dignity and honor.

I want you to know that Morgan LOVED YOU more than words can say. I remember Morgan coming up this summer and her raving about you after working at Carilion. She was so proud of you and impressed by how vital you are to the company. Morgan got to add this experience to her understanding and respect for you and this allowed her to appreciate you even more. Morgan lived every day of her life knowing that her Papa loved her and would do anything for her which is more than many people can say.

She is beyond pain now and her love and spirit will continue to give you strength and help you through the difficulties left in her wake. Even though Morgan is gone, you will always be the father of TWO children. You always did your best to understand and support us both. Know that I am loving you now for both of us and when you need the same support and understanding you have always given, I am here.

Happy Father's Day, 2010

Love,

Alex and Morgan

June 19, 2010   *Poem for Dan*

Mourn no mo

For Mogo

You don't stoppa
Being a girl's papa
Just coz she's dead
Get that outa your head
Your daddy chore
Has expanded more
No longer tending boo boo knee
Now you're creating legacy
Of goodness
And kindness
And strength
For the world to see
While still parenting Alex and partnering me
Bless you for all the fathering you've done
For our precious daughter, our precious son
Your ability
And constancy
Continue to amaze
Even in these hardest days
That I never thought would be ours to live
We must still have more to give
I promise that we'll find a way
To resurrect joy someday

Father's Day 2010

—∞—

June 20, 2010   *Acclimate*

Evil does exist and life can be savage at times. Despite that, I know love will persist and goodness continues. I hold fast to this truth as I stumble in sadness and fear, knowing my sight will acclimate to the darkness soon and I'll learn to navigate this shadow land with ease.

I wish I could hurry the process along. I yearn for ease and a lightening of our burden. But grief has its own clock and doesn't seem to care about my time frame at all. I believe healing could occur more readily if I got out of the way and allowed it to unfold.

My knee jerk is to meet a problem with strength, shoulder it, attack it, wrestle it, oppose it. Regrettably, there's no dominating Death or her sister, Grief. I want to be a force for good, but realize that force is impotent here. To process Morgan's death in a healthy way, I must develop a whole new survival skill-set based on submission and surrender. Dan will confirm that those attributes are pretty foreign to my character.

Am being forced to change and grow and yield. I hope my pig-headed resistance will be short-lived and I learn to stop throwing myself against the rock and instead flow around it.

Intellectually, I understand, but my anguished heart still can't stop screaming WHY?

My little Mogo,

241

—⚬⚬—

June 21, 2010   *Motivator*

We were in Charlottesville yesterday to acknowledge the passing of 8 months since Morgan's abduction/murder. We are getting so tired of beating this drum, trying to incite vigilance in this pretty Charlottesville community where a psychopathic murderer still walks.

This killer enjoys violence. He has worked his way up to the top of the predator food chain, killing humans for sport. The exhilaration and power he seeks through murder will not easily be satisfied by lesser crimes. If not caught, he will re-offend, hurt/kill someone else's daughter.

That belief makes me frantic for an arrest. Not a quest for justice, or closure, or even punishment, but so that some other sweet girl be spared his blood lust.

That's a hell of a motivator. Even if we're tired, even if people think we should get over it and go away, we persist. It is too late for Morgan, but I can't give up on the next girl.

241

—⚬⚬—

June 23, 2010 *Personal*

PERSONAL AD –
MORGAN DANA HARRINGTON

Beautiful, smart, funny
20-year-old female, single
college student
Metallica fan, murder victim

Seeks JUSTICE/ARREST/
CONVICTION

Call VSP with information
On Morgan's case @
434-352-3467

241

—⟋⟍—

June 28, 2010 *Reckoning*

Note to a monster:

Listen up. There is karma or fate or destiny. Evil may rule for a while, but eventually, inevitably, without fail, the pendulum swings and your reign will be over. I'm ready. Your clock is ticking down. Any time now, good will prevail.

I understand this in a visceral way, just like I understand you. We are obscenely linked opposite mirror images. I created Morgan's life force and birthed her. You destroyed that life and murdered her. I felt her first faint fetal movements. You felt her death rigors. I knew Morgan as an embryo. You knew her as a corpse.

That corpse will not rest. Morgan wants justice. I hear her whispering in the ears and softening the hearts of those who help you hide. They don't like what you've become. Your call to violence has become a blood lust and you are a monster. They grow frightened, knowing the truth will out. A day of reckoning is coming!

Morgan 241

—⟋⟍—

July 12, 2010   *Noxema*

Back from the beach trip. It was our first vacation without Morgan. It was hard, especially for Dan. Both of them shared a love of the surf and waves and would stay immersed for hours. I miss seeing them play in the waves laughing. I miss watching freckles bloom on her nose. I miss anointing pinked sunburned skin with Noxzema. I miss combing out her tangled hair. I miss sand in the bed. I miss Morgan.

As you can see my surrender and submit got up and went. I am back, stuck in the whys and what ifs and have lost my "it is" perspective. Suffering has unmoored and set us adrift at sea, a sea of tears whose very salinity will give us the buoyancy we need to stay afloat.

I don't love where we are but still believe that we have an opportunity to learn from the master teacher, pain, if only we can survive the lesson.

241

—⁂—

July 16, 2010   *Back to school*

Re-entry from our week at the beach has been hard. You can lose yourself in the vastness of the sea and drown the memories that fight for attention. Since returning we have all been on the skids, not sure exactly why. Could be that the cumulative grief load has finally grown into an incapacitating, crippling mass.

I have lost some of the emotional equilibrium that I had gathered and find myself again rapidly cycling several times a day. At moments I'm standing on a shaky platform of OK and then am seized by despair. Today's trigger was walking into a store featuring back to school/decorate your dorm stuff. It took my breath away. Had to jettison my list and leave.

It's not that I begrudge others the pleasure of this nesting and planning, rather it's that the notebooks and mouse pads and study lamps bring floods of memories of how Morgan and I planned and shopped to launch her into her "grown up" life at Virginia Tech. Hopes and dreams for Morgan's life were ended by a savage murder.

I watch young fresh faced girls and their mamas searching for the perfect set of sheets for college. My experience of that shared activity is tainted by my overlay, because my memory is of cutting Morgan's perfect college sheets off her bed and bagging them as scent items for dogs. That thought cascade pulls me right back down again into the rabbit hole of WHY?

It's a tough place we've been forced into, an ugly world of sadness /death/ DNA/ and murder. This is where Morgan's death has taken us and so we must follow as well as we can. We are able to soldier on because the love, support, and prayers of many holds us up. The past 9 months have been full of uncertainty and darkness but we seek to give birth to truth and to find answers, not for retribution but to protect the next girl. I'm not looking for satisfaction. What I'm after is safety, so that another precious life is not ended by this evil.

241

—∿—

July 21, 2010 *Surrender*

What is compelling about loss is that we know that everyone will at some time be challenged by its touch. Folks are looking for a road map, not answers per se, but the suggestion of a route to take, to traverse that rough terrain when their turn inevitably comes up.

When disaster like Morgan's murder occurs, your life is shattered. You become addled and disoriented. Logic and experience no longer point to a direction you can follow. That is precisely the place where you can either choose to break or surrender: when you are so overwhelmed by grief that you throw it in and yield. This is the point where transformation and grace happens.

If I have any advice or wisdom to pass along to others confronting devastating loss, it would be to surrender to this mystery of faith more easily than I have done. I have stubbornly clung to my charade of control and wrestle often with "why" and "how can it be?"

I find my bearings and comfort only when I step on the fragile tenuous platform of my faith, persistently returning to the knowledge that God is in this experience somewhere. Only good can come from this because God is here. Trust that God's plan is good. Surely the presence is in this place, love is in this place, healing is in this place; renewal and growth are in this place.

I am finding a path though I still have a long way to go. I can sense that I have grown, not grateful for the experience yet, but finding some acceptance.

Life is intended for good. Don't succumb to doubt and fear. God will take care of us. This may not be what we wanted, but something good will come from it, and has come from it.

241

—∿—

June 23, 2010   *Just ask Morgan*

I am dancing around the realization that I have allowed the shadow of Morgan's death to obscure much of the joy and reverence in my daily life. It is hard to dispel the darkness, but am I honoring our shiny girl with this pervasive gloom? I think not.

Every day we are alive is a gift (just ask Morgan). Notice it, give thanks, plug back into the gratitude/positive circuit. Count the blessings as they present.

Because of the torrent of kindness and generosity we have received, we remember that goodness will prevail and life is worth living. We reap such love from our community in the midst of pain that we believe and somehow continue on. Thanks to so many who carry us.

241

—⚊—

June 27, 2011   *Grace notes*

Goodness, things have to lighten up soon. I am about at the limits of my strength and ability to process information. I am just back from a quick trip to NYC to visit Alex. It feels like I have been in constant motion since returning to Africa—to NYC twice, to D.C., to Charlottesville, to North Carolina—spinning like a top at times. I have been traveling so much that I'm getting disoriented when I open the fridge and think, But I know I just bought milk. Where is it? Oh, that was another fridge. Much of my busyness is to stop the despair that Dan and Alex slide into during my two weeks away in Africa. We have all become like delicate plants that wither quickly when nurturing and tending is withdrawn.

So I am on the circuit to do my Mama nurturing, leaving filled refrigerators, clean laundry, and order in my wake. That is a particularly hard task to do in New York City where I have to cart the fixings of every meal through the streets for several blocks and then up three flights of stairs to Alex's apartment. I found myself considering meals dependent on their weight. Somehow, I couldn't get Alex to buy into a dinner of rice cakes, popcorn, and marshmallows. Pity, it would have been so easy—and light! It is funny to figure out what value you add. I see that mine is to provide sanctuary to those I love, easing things up a bit.

This is a nice gig to have and pretty intuitive for me. I know how to make the daily grind recede and the sense of home emerge. When Dan and Alex fall in the door, I can be there to catch them with the sustenance of food and music and love all around. Then, they are able to take that nexus of calm and use it as

119

a foundation to take on the world—the next day. With my caring, I chip away at some of the anguish from your death and the incessant demands of work.

The habit of my joy is so easily forgotten and most difficult to rekindle. We have definitely lost our way on this—we have got the work side of the equation down solidly, but the pleasure/reward part is missing since your murder, Morgan. I believe that the way out is to add the grace notes, wherever possible, and to guard the space where contentment might grow. Exuding joy into your life is like the letting down of milk; it cannot be forced, but creating an environment of serenity allows the nurture to flow. We need to pay attention to this process and help it along. Otherwise, I fear we are at risk of essentially becoming collateral victims of Morgan's killer—alive, but without a life.

No way, no how will I let him inflict further damage on us; we will work it out. I happened on a phrase that resonated whose idea I want to use for our triangulated family: "post-traumatic growth." It is possible—it even has a name! Morgan, help us conjure this reality.

241
Mama

—⁓—

July 23, 2010   *Catalyst*

Today is the golf tournament to benefit the building of the Morgan Harrington Educational Wing at OMNI Village in Zambia, Africa. Such a courageous and clever triumph over darkness to continue to wrestle good out of Morgan's tragic death.

Because of events like this, Morgan's life has created a legacy of goodness that continues to impact the world. To be truthful, Morgan's posthumous achievements may actually supersede what she was likely to accomplish if she had been allowed to live. Ironic, isn't it?

As a parent I am so grateful, so happy, that Morgan's murderer has not been able to erase her completely from the world. Morgan chose a profession in education and she will, in fact, be part of educating and teaching many. Morgan Harrington will not be a poster child for rape, abduction and murder. Instead, Morgan will be remembered as a catalyst for teaching and care given to deserving students in the United States and Africa, as well. We are so grateful to all who have helped us snatch this treasure out of the ashes of our Morgan.

241

—⁓—

July 26, 2010   *Erin*

Dearest Mokie,

This was a weekend to remember, memories to cherish. Not the manner of celebrating your 21ˢᵗ birthday that I had ever anticipated, but unexpectedly wonderful and joy-filled, regardless.

Erin, little Erin, masterfully orchestrated your Morgan Harrington Memorial Golf Tournament. What a friend she remains to you!

It was fun and crazy and hot as blazes and it rained and that didn't matter one bit. There was great food and cake (Papa thanks you much) and a bubble machine and tears and, Morgan, love permeated every moment. Papa careened around Hanging Rock Golf Course in a cart desperately searching for the turn signal and/or cruise control. I quickly gave up my co-pilot seat when I realized he wasn't really clear that it was not a bumper car. Another new place you have taken us.

Your memorial at the bridge in Charlottesville had balloons and more cake, and prayers and laughter and I lay on the sidewalk after and did the ugly cry and stroked the pictures of your face. Somehow that spot has the feeling of sacred ground to us now.

Our neighborhood had that sacred aspect as we looked out at the 21 luminaries around our yard that loved ones had placed in your memory. Dan crawled back into bed after a 4 a.m. Kirby pit stop and nudged me to report "Morgan's birthday candles are still burning bright".

And you did, my little Morgan, you burned so bright and shiny. Perhaps such incandescence is meant to last only for a short while.

Although I don't understand the place we live now, I do know that the tsunami of love we have received in the last few days leaves us breathless and humble. If we can find enough faith to let this flow over us and not block it, the fact that you were, that Morgan Harrington lived, will really change the world.

An amazing meteor ride you are taking us on as you leave, Morgan. We are holding tight. Take us where you will. Love abides.

241

July 28, 2010   *Morgan's car*

Perspective sometimes flows along smoothly and other times chinks and jumps like gears on a tank. We had that little click of perspective change this week with Morgan's car.

Until recently, seeing Morgan's car parked in the driveway was a comfort for us, a comfort with a few barbs, to be truthful. I'd drive up and the reflexive lift," Oh, Morgan is home" was nice, but too quickly followed by the reality that no, she is not and never will be here again. Even so, it was good to see Morgan's car here for 9 months. It gave us a sense that things were where they should be.

These are the games you play with yourself. "It's okay--everything is in its right place. Oh yeah, except your daughter, but not to worry. Every other thing is exactly where it should be." It only took 9 months, 2 jumps, and 1 battery replacement for me to get it. Alright, I can let go of this too.

It makes us sad, another piece of Morgan to let go of. Now we have an empty driveway to go with the empty bedroom upstairs. Rather than sit in that sorrow we have gifted Morgan's car in a way that will lift and transform another.

Perhaps it is evidence of healing that we are able to tune in again to the wisdom of flow and be willing to relinquish things that have served their purpose. Are we supposed to extrapolate from this some insight about Morgan and the meaning of her life? She came, she lived, and left after she had fulfilled her purpose? A wedge to open us up and unravel our tangles and then knit us back together into new, tighter, more complex and intricate cloth?

241

—⚊⚊—

August 2, 2010   *Vestiges*

Morgan,

We cocooned you in love for 20 years. Was it enough? Did we manage to cram a life's worth into that short allotment?

I feel cheated and pretty pissed off that we were robbed of the joy of your presence for the rest of our lives. It is selfish I know, we wanted you here with us until we up and died; but fate turned the tables on that scenario. How can it be?

The vestiges of you that we rejoice in are getting fainter. I go into your room to conjure you and try to sniff your scent from t-shirts. Even your closet is losing the essence of Morgan and smells disappointing, flat, sort of generic now. I guess empty is the right word.

The tangible Morgan dissipates and yet the connection persists. Selfishly, I am not content with a monologue. Morgan give us something, anything, to break through the barrier. We are all wishing for something, a big sign from you. Morgan, how about putting the 2 4 1 dots on the moon for a night? Just once!

241

—⚋—

August 4, 2010   *Tropism*

It is not fair! Life is just not fair. When I have that reaction to Morgan's murder I remind myself that we were never promised fairness; what we were promised though is the strength and the tools needed to overcome any obstacle.

We are developing that strength because we have been able to lean heavily on so many that we move forward. Family, both biologic and chosen, will always back you up; and our dear, reliable family have made the path so much easier.

Life has always been precarious. We don't realize the myriad disasters and catastrophes we squeak by every day. Like the haphazard steps of a toddler stumbling around the living room narrowly missing the sharp corner on the coffee table – over and over again, sooner or later, an inevitable wrong step ends with a head bump and hurt and tears.

So it is with life; you get knocked over but don't or can't resign yourself to stay with crawling because walking is too dangerous. We are programmed in the fiber of our being to get back up and try again. I think of our resilience as tropism of the soul: we keep turning towards the light. It is what we are meant to do.

I reject brokenness in our life. I acknowledge a broken heart but am determined that the shattering will only open this heart to experience more love. We honor Morgan, not with withered lives, but through glorious triumphant flowering.

Can we do it?

241

—⚋—

August 9, 2010   *Frantic*

Flat busted and tired! Some of it is emotional, but primarily I am aware that I have overspent myself physically. We moved some of Morgan's apartment furnishings to Alex in New York City this week. A 14-foot truck and Manhattan rush hour is pretty scary; then if you make it there you have to unload and carry all up numerous stairs--a challenge to be sure. It was worth all the effort, though, because settling our remaining child comfortably and safely in his environment was balm for the soul.

Soon though, somehow we have to ratchet down the pace we are keeping; it just isn't sustainable much longer. All three of us are running full tilt, like dogs with a string of tin cans attached to their tails, the cacophony scaring us to run ever faster. We approach the end of our reserves so it's about time to slow down and reconsider. We need to figure out why we must run so fast.

In fear? Of what? The worst has already happened.

Morgan has been murdered. Why run now?

Are we fueling this frantic pace, doing it to ourselves because it distracts us from the painful void in our lives from Morgan's death? Is it better to run to exhaustion than turn and face the full brunt of sadness? This method of self-distraction will bring self-destruction if we don't rein it in. We need some quiet and stillness to reflect on our profound loss and the sorrow we feel.

I relish the little reassuring signs that signal things will be ok, eventually. I had one as we left New York in that 14 foot truck: bumper to bumper cars into the Lincoln tunnel, horns blaring, confusing lights and traffic patterns, and cops banging on the side of the truck. I glanced up at the back of the semi ahead of us and saw the logo "MORGAN" right in front of our windshield. It was going to be ok. Morgan will lead us through the Lincoln Tunnel. I sat back in the seat, stopped clutching the armrest and let out my breath. Thankful to realize that even in this hole underground, despite my fear, despite all appearances, we were being led into the sunlight.

241

—∞—

August 12, 2010   *Sprinkles*

It is so silly the things that get under your skin. In cleaning cabinets today, I discarded "Morgan items", things that no longer have any relevance to our lives, Brown sugar, she was the one who loved to mix up batches of chocolate chip cookies. We, our family, have no need for brown sugar anymore. I was cool with that, but sprinkles – that was hard. How ridiculous! With everything we have had to let go of, to mourn sprinkles leaving the kitchen cabinet. But until it's gone you don't fully realize the impact, the whimsy, and the fun that a daughter brings to lighten life's gray tones.

I know it isn't about sprinkles; it's about the loss of joy that Morgan brought to our existence. We have survived Morgan's death; but we are not sure we see the rationale/value in surviving her ongoing absence. It looks like much work, with little joy. It is imperative that we find a way to celebrate the life we have, even in the face of pain. The path seems so murky though – Morgan help us find a way.

241

August 16, 2010   *It is*

My mind fills with a clamor of struggle:
Why Morgan? so wrong/but it is.
Not fair, why us?/It is.
She was so fine had so much yet to give / it is.
We will never see her children, we won't feel her soft hand on our faces as we die / it is.
Surrender sucks.
Stubbornly, insistently, incessantly I want to keep crashing against the rock of WHY?
How can this horrific murder be the destiny of Morgan Harrington? / It is.
God help us!

241

August 17, 2010   *Rip tides*

Suffering. There's plenty of it to go around though it is largely ignored and perhaps undervalued. I believe that suffering provides opportunity for strengthening and transformation. As humans we will all have moments of exquisite suffering and pain. Figuring out how to deal with it is a necessary skill. Interesting that suffering isn't even much depicted in our popular culture. As if the only responses to tragedy are rage and dysfunction, you fight it or are broken by it. Another, more challenging option is to incorporate the pain of suffering into the matrix of your life and to use it.

If we deny that suffering occurs, how do we learn to suffer with grace? Suffering perhaps exists to tire us enough of our own will and be willing to surrender to the mystery of transformation. We must learn to choose willingness, not willfulness. I cannot resist the reality of this pain. It's foolish even to try.

Suffering is like one of the rip tides in Avon, North Carolina, on the Outer Banks. If you flail against the rip tide, it will whisk you off and drown you. Many go that way. To survive, you must keep your wits, jettison fear, and do the counter-intuitive thing—go with the current. Eventually, you will make it ashore, not where you began, not where you planned to end up, but further along the beach. Still breathing.

241

———

August 20, 2010   *Abomination*

Early on, we chose to share our story, share our pain. This was therapeutic for us in some ways; like the guy who will lift up his shirt (with little encouragement) to show his puckered surgical scar. The retelling helps integrate this massive body insult into his reality. We have told the story of Morgan's murder at the drop of a hat for some of the same reasons. In the recitation we hear ourselves and begin to accept the unfathomable: Morgan was brutally murdered.

The intentionality of it bothers me so. How/why could anyone hurt her? On purpose?

If someone had run over her, I would be trying to give forgiveness for a terrible accident. I know Morgan was killed deliberately. I am not in a place of withholding forgiveness. I haven't gotten that far. My mind still cannot accept, cannot conceive of a reality where someone could actually kill.

What an abomination.

Mogo 241

August 25, 2010   *Cyber crime*

Feeling the lash today
Of those who tell me "go away"

Seems our story's getting sort of stale
Time to hear another tale

They enjoyed a vicarious thriller,
Chatting about your vicious killer,
But now it's old hat, so
Enough, enough of that.

What I thought they came to see
Was how to act with dignity,
When life hits its fiercest blow
But they want a reality show
With plots and yelling,
Drama most compelling.

Don't they get that this is our life. That we live every day?
Wish we could make it go away.

Morgan, you're just as dead as you were before—
Pity it doesn't interest anymore.

Sorry the story's lost its cachet, but it's the story we must tell
To put a killer in a cell.

So if you really want to give advice
And make snarky comments that aren't nice,

Fine, and welcome to the "game"—it's great—

Admission is pricey—it's somebody's fate.

Is it your son or your daughter you'll throw on the plate?

241

—∞—

August 29, 2010   *Wrestling thoughts of death*

I honestly do not understand the death avoidance in our society. Some folks, even ones who know me well, can barely make eye contact or mumble a few words to me now that I have this new, unasked for, unwanted, role as a mother to a murdered girl.

Open dialogue about death is rare. We utilize euphemisms to try and soften the pain. I prefer plain speaking, with clear words. Morgan has not "passed on" or "been called to heaven". She was murdered, and is dead. I don't like that fact one bit, but I can acclimate to the harsh reality, given time. If folks only allow me the platitudes that they are comfortable with, I will never learn to accommodate to our loss. I will be left floundering forever in a quagmire of well-intentioned fluffy double-speak.

It flabbergasts me that we watch graphic clinical scenarios for all kinds of products on TV, but any meaningful practical talk of death is still taboo. Truth is, death is really OK. It can even be heart-wrenchingly beautiful.

I know this raw grandeur from participating in the leave taking of many. In particular, the death of Jacqueline Haensli, my beloved sister, was a tutorial on the power of courage and grace. Witnessing death strips us of pretense and forces us to consider the most fundamental core of our beliefs. The frank and honest contemplation of death is necessary, even healthy, for each of us to do.

Coming to terms with the rough spots is where you mine the bedrock foundation of your own faith.

Every single one of us will have at least one up-close and personal encounter with death. It is pivotal that we come to some acceptance and understanding of that process. If I can present as transparent and undefended, then others can drop their facade. We can connect, and discover that neither of us is alone. Identity released from role yields intimacy.

Death is a stark, harsh landscape, like a desert, and like a desert, it has its own surprising, bright beauty. Stripping the extraneous nonessentials away from something exposes an innate, poignant singularity.

Death, not the sugar-coatings of finery or fortune, reveals the incandescent spirit housed in the body. I do realize, though, that the dying process isn't easy, nor often very pretty. Much like birth, death provokes primitive, genuine, fundamental emotions. It is messy, sloppy, painful. Regardless, I want those feelings, every single shred of them.

I am not sure if I am wired strangely, but like a dog, I want to roll in it. I want to experience every aspect of Morgan's death. I want to feel her bones, wear her shoes, and sniff her clothes. Not sure if I am trying to imprint the last of her, indelibly in my mind, or if I indulge in such intimacy to try and have the reality of her absence penetrate my disbelief.

It was my privilege to watch her come into the world. Somehow it is also my duty to contemplate her death. I will try to witness the end of Morgan's life with the same clarity and understanding as I did her birth on July 24, 1989. I will cherish and acknowledge Morgan's spirit now that she is dead, to the same degree I did when she had a body.

How could I do otherwise? She was our precious child.

241

———

August 30, 2010   *Canaries*

I am enraged and amazed by the tolerance for violence and acceptance of crimes against the weaker members of our society, women and children in America. Is it really OK? Are we still just expendable goods?

Beware! I believe the numerous injured and murdered women and children are the coal mine canaries of our times; delicate creatures whose deaths indicate a lethal toxic presence in our midst. They are a barometer of evil. Take note, hear the alarm and address the underlying problem of pervasive violence. Don't just step over the corpse of the next lifeless golden creature and say, "funny, another dead bird."

If you keep doing that, ignoring sentinel events, sooner or later the lethal emanations of violence will have fingers wrapped around your throat, choking your breath away - all because you didn't listen, turned aside, couldn't be bothered, ignored the signals because it couldn't happen to you.

The fluttering wings of coal mine canaries in their death rigors have become deafening. Can't you hear the clamor? Please listen, take heed, there is poison here. Find another path or risk your very lives.

Mogo – 241

———

September 1, 2010   *Hologram*

We are really smack up against a decision point now. We know we can survive the devastating loss of Morgan; we have done so for 10+ months. The question now is we must decide if we even want to. Do we choose to LIVE again? Not just to eke out an existence but to actually embrace life? It's hard; part of us is still numb and asleep to the rhythms and energy of a normal life. We walk a stumbling gait, with one foot in the world of the living and the other firmly planted in the land of the dead. Eventually, soon, we will have to choose and commit to one or the other.

Our friends and family cajole, and beckon, and even bully us to return to a more normal way of living. Haven't we suffered enough yet? The pain quota has been met. Is it time to be happy? No. There is still imbalance in the equation. We cannot be breathing and have suffered as much as Morgan did. How do you wall off or neutralize the too vivid imaginings of her death throes? How do you stop superimposing the hologram of Morgan's skull on every young face you see?

This reality, our horror, is wrong. Morgan should be at Virginia Tech, settling into her apartment for her senior year, stocking the fridge and calling Dan for money and help reconciling her check book, or maybe in line at the VT bookstore waiting to buy yet another Hokie hoodie. But she is chapwa, finished, no more, over. We feel finished too. You know, there's not even a word for our role. It is that aberrant, that abhorrent. Children whose parents die are called orphans. Parents whose children die have no special name. They are called nothing – they have nothing.

That's what we feel. That's what we are, nothing. Trying so hard to find a way out of this wasteland of nothing and be called survivors.

241

—⟫⟩⟨⟨—

September 3, 2010   *In plain sight*

I have spent a lot of time these last 8! months contemplating secrets. Some secrets are information intentionally withheld; other secrets are hidden by happenstance or coincidence. A tricky one is the secret we keep from ourselves because we kind of see it but know it is ugly and cannot bear to confront it – yet.

A really great way to conceal something and keep it secret is to hide it in plain sight. I did this often with Morgan and Alex's gifts at Christmas. The kids were masters at searching out presents that I had carefully hidden and squirreled away. Eventually, I learned that the best place to hide secret things is in plain sight where they could be easily overlooked, seemingly obvious spots where they blended in and their edges were a little blurry but fully hidden or obscured. Those definitely were the most successful hiding places.

This is just how the murderer in Charlottesville is escaping detection, by hiding in plain sight. He is a little off, his edges blurred, but he can pass if you only glance quickly and then look away. When a predator is walking among you, hiding in plain sight, you should not be so inattentive. You must be alert, really evaluating everyone around you. Always have an exit strategy in place. When the hairs on your neck raise and your skin starts to crawl, take note, get out, call the police, and we'll have him.

I believe that secrets have a season, like fruit. The secret of who killed Morgan Harrington is ready to be plucked and broken open. It is so cloyingly-over ripe that it is starting to smell.

241

—※—

September 7, 2010   *Holiday*

We have to find a relationship with Morgan that transcends the inconvenient fact of her death. I am not sure how to do that yet.

Healing demands inclusion of memories and hopefully integrating them into a new reality/life. Trying to accomplish this and winnowing through our memory cascade of life with Morgan so quickly derails into wallowing in grief and loss. We must somehow learn to mute that pain circuit so we can build on the foundation of love and remembrances we have and move our triangulated family forward.

I realize that we honor Morgan most completely when we live in a full and gracious way. I just can't get on the happy track though; we are working at it but it is still almost as if we feel that being happy would signify that we had not loved Morgan enough.

The suddenness of violent death is disorienting. It makes you go a little crazy, so that sometimes we act in a really counterintuitive way. This weekend is a perfect example. Moths are drawn to the flame; we are not luna moths but lunatic moths, perversely drawn to where Morgan's flame was snuffed out, mesmerized by the blackness of shadows as we quest for justice. A holiday weekend, we could have gone anywhere, but we had to open the wound again and found ourselves drawn, compelled to Morgan's Bridge in Charlottesville.

There we flutter around the void of your absence, Morgan, and wish so hard we could escape the call to darkness and be pulled instead by vestiges of light. Shiny girl, show us a way.

241

—∞—

September 10, 2010   *Fatigue*

We met with the Virginia State Police today. In the vast wasteland of our loss and grief we look to them for answers. We have become increasingly angry with the lack of progress in the investigation of Morgan's murder.

I work myself into a tizzy the night before these scheduled meetings with LE; planning the knuckle-rapping I will deliver all around. But when they walk into the house and I look into their eyes, I can see their fatigue and frustration. It penetrates me to clearly see Ed and Dino bracing themselves to receive an angry diatribe from me. These are good men, working diligently to the fullest of their abilities, to find resolution to the horrific murder of Morgan.

I realize that the legitimate target of the consuming raging inferno of our anger about Morgan's death is the person who abducted her, raped her, butchered her, and abandoned her as refuse in a hay field.

Anything that distracts us from focusing squarely on that evil crime and criminal is wasted energy. So I am learning patience and surrender – hard lessons.

241

—∞—

September 13, 2010   *Euphemisms*

Our struggle with processing Morgan's death is complicated by a duality of purpose. A murder creates this dichotomy. On one hand, we must submit and learn to accept the fact that Morgan is no more, her life is over. We must relinquish our hopes and dreams – surrender. At the very same time we must fight, stir ourselves to sound the alarm and amp up attention, concern, and action because a killer is still on the loose and will most likely harm or kill again.

It is grueling and exhausting to struggle through the sludge and weight of our sadness and then try to overcome the established status quo which tries to soothe and minimize the vicious act that took Morgan's life and the actor who poses continued danger.

There is an entrenched culture of violence and victimization against women and children in this country. Period. The extent of the ravaging has been ignored and allowed for some time. The very language used to describe assault and abduction seeks to minimize the inherent savagery of the acts committed. In my verbiage, Morgan was not "missing" – she was snatched. Things did not get "out of hand" – Morgan was assaulted and raped. Morgan did not "pass away" – she was murdered and slaughtered.

Soothing tones and soft language are appropriate when the evil monster is make-believe in a child's bedtime story, not when he walks in your town.

I am reminded here on the cusp of the 9/11 anniversary, that the buildings' occupants were soothed and directed back to their offices, back to business as usual, back to their deaths.

Be alert! You cannot queue up like placid sheep when evil is loose in the land.

In sheep's clothing, one Canis lupus, a wild and rabid timber wolf, now queues alongside.

241

—⚊—

September 22, 2010   Stains

Coming back from our trip to NYC to visit Alex and taking hold of my own home and settling in again, I keep thinking: wouldn't it be great if our lives were more like laundry. Such a wonderful process; the stretched out, sweat-stained, frankly odorous stuff of living is miraculously reconstituted. A do-over! With reasonable minor effort all the dirty/unkempt/tangled/rough items we contact are cleansed and deodorized and folded back into their original configurations; a sweet-smelling rescue.

Life in general and our lives in particular don't usually work out this way. I wish we were laundry with a fragrant transfiguration looming. Somehow our reality cannot be folded into nice straight little piles any longer, even with HUGE effort and work. It just ain't happening. After almost 1 year of struggling to find justice for Morgan Harrington's murder, we are left with bloodstained clothing on our laps. We wish so much that life indeed really was like the miracle of laundry.

241
P.S. bloodstains never come out

September 29, 2010   *Fake*

Grief is not an all or nothing process, like we are ok, or we are in despair. There is a lot of wiggle room, not frank polarity which would be so much simpler. There are moments when we all do well, and there are times we fake it like crazy and it is sort of convinces. The problem is that when you have to do that, fake it, to make our pain tolerable/acceptable to others and self – it is just exhausting.

I am tired of growing, and trying, and following the rough path. I want it smooth and easy for a bit; we are due. I am just confounded that this is ours to walk – so damn hard. Then I remember the journey our daughter took. Morgan's path ended with her shattered body strewn in a field and I am shamed by my weakness and my fatigue and I find motivation to soldier on for a little more. We must find some answers, some justice before we can put this down.

241

—ᴍ—

October 4, 2010   *Baby lock*

A psychic 2 x 4 lurks around the house, waiting to catch you unaware so it can deliver a smack. It caught me square and leveled me last night. I was scrabbling in an unaccustomed cabinet for a little used pan and I couldn't get the door open. Without even thinking, on automatic, my hands knew to pull only a half inch and insert index finger to depress the plastic spring mechanism of the baby lock. We tried to keep Morgan so safe from harm, hot burners, sharp knives, fast cars, influenza, cavities. The mantra was always protect, protect, protect. How could we ever have imagined we needed to protect her from murder? Unbelievable to me still. Ridiculous that a silly little plastic baby cabinet lock has lasted longer than the baby it was installed to protect – our beloved and grievously mourned baby girl, Morgan Dana Harrington.

241

—ᴍ—

October 10, 2010   *Bird strikes*

We have lived in this house for almost 20 years. Morgan came to this house as a babe in arms and learned how to walk here with her soft baby feet, tip-toeing around.

In the considerable span of our occupation we have had only a few episodes of bird interaction. I think I can remember two or three times a small sparrow got through the screen door to our screened deck and had to be redirected back to the doorway and freedom. That is really about it for the bird contact here. I do put out seed for the pleasure of watching the birds eat and realize, as I do, the decadence of this ritual as human beings in Zambia would be most pleased to have the sustenance of this throw away food, millet and sunflower gruel.

That has been the extent of my interaction with birds here. I feed, I watch with pleasure as they eat (in truth the squirrels mostly eat, but they are beautiful and worth watching also). About two months ago, it started happening – bird strikes, frequent and relentless! Mourning doves slamming into the windows of the house. Pressed on the glass over my kitchen sink is the imprint of a cushioned downy bird's breast and outstretched wings – an otherworldly Rorschach of desperation.

At first I felt uneasy that it happened so much; birds pelting the house with their bodies. I would buff off the smudges their impact left on every window. I never find any bodies under the window's point of contact but our house is festooned by the marks. Our living room window has the 2 4 1 dots on it in the form of reflective discs; five bird strikes prints now circle the 2 4 1 emblem.

This phenomenon was becoming disturbing to me until a wise friend explained, "of course it is happening, and no, it is not Morgan at the window crashing into the glass seeikng re-entry, but it is a type of Morgan energy still present and reactive. You cannot stop yourself from the heart cry of the searching and pleading you put out as Morgan's parents any more than the birds can stop themselves from responding. The visceral gut level screeching summons you emanate must be answered by the universe in some way".

I see bird strikes. I understand and am grateful but wish instead that the very rocks and trees would rise up and move to spit out the abomination, the lethal poison, of a monster who wrung the life from our golden bird, Morgan Dan Harrington.

241

—∞—

October 17, 2010   *Gil's bridge talk*

Nine months. It took nine months to create all the parts that made Morgan Dana Harrington. It took nine months to assemble all the parts that made the composite of a murderer also.

Charlottesville, it is time to deliver, time to labor and work to expel this criminal who has found safe harbor in your community. There are folks here who know and shelter him.

I want justice, yes. But my motivation is not revenge. It is safety. He is a serial offender. He will reoffend.

You have a fresh crop of naïve young students coming to Charlottesville in the next few months. Find and remove the threat of this predator before the next girl is taken.

Morgan was a vivacious, witty, beautiful girl, not a semen-stained rag to be tossed in the field like garbage. She was a human being.

He is not. He is a monster. He is the back-to-school killer. Please, Charlottesville, help us find Sketch. He is lethal.

241

—◊◊◊—

December 9, 2010   *Cold*

This Christmas season has been especially sharp for me. I couldn't figure out exactly why. It wasn't just the feeling that we are so outside the celebratory jolly-ness of the holidays. That exclusion is a bit sad, but not painful. It finally dawned on me yesterday; it's the cold, the pervasive bitter cold. Last year, Morgan's body had not been found by this time. We desperately clung to the fantasy that Morgan was alive somewhere and each cold night or snowfall was a torture as we imagined Morgan exposed to the elements and suffering. She was indeed exposed to the elements, but her suffering was long past. I am so very grateful to have that knowledge.

There is a PTSD quality to our feelings right now. We're cycling fast. Initially, shock and disbelief are like insulation that protect you from feeling too much. As those feelings have dissipated we've been hit full on with tremendous emotion over Morgan's death this winter. The extremely low temperatures and strong winds also leave me breathless with eyes and nose streaming every time I dash outside. The sensation of secretions pouring down my face has me constantly feeling like I am recovering from a crying jag and it hurts like before.

It seems that the tissues of my eyes, the skin of my cheeks don't differentiate between wind-driven tears and tears of heartbreak. Both leave me spent.

People want us to get over it. Hell, we want to get over it. But we are different people now, irrevocably changed by the murder of our daughter. The constellations of friendships are reforming based upon others' comfort level with our discomfort. That's OK. I've heard "get better or be bitter" and I don't think we are bitter, but know we are not better, at least not yet. We are working hard and I am immensely proud that we have survived the first year of our separation from Morgan. It may be that as those years stack up, the loss won't feel as sharp, though I doubt it.

241

—⁓—

January 12, 2011   *Chocolates*

It is very slow, finding your way through a minefield like the holidays. We did so well! we had some genuine moments of joy, even though there were also many crying times. There is a lot of pain in discarding family traditions that are fractured for us without Morgan taking her part in them.

Like: Morgan was always the best at deciphering the treasure hunt clues for the "biggest" gift. We won't/can't play that game anymore.

Like: Morgan loved those chocolate crinkle cookies that you refrigerate and roll in powdered sugar. I would make them only at Christmas time. Morgan had a sixth sense of exactly when, and inevitably she would find the refrigerated dough and would eat the majority before we could get the cookies baked. We won't/can't make that recipe anymore.

Like: Morgan had what appeared to be a giant green scrunchie with bells all over it. She would ask our dog Kirby to wear his Jingle Bell Necklace on Christmas mornings. Kirby is sort of schizoid and afraid of his own shadow, so you can imagine how dubious his response to his Christmas attire was. Morgan thought he looked so good in green, and she soothed him so he could handle his fashion. We won't/can't do that anymore. (Kirby is profoundly grateful for the reprieve, but I miss the silliness.)

Like: Morgan was notorious for taking one little nibble from most of the chocolates in a sampler, and then putting them back, in her quest for her favorite caramels. Many repetitions of "if you bite it, you eat it" made her change her ways. Instead, to get around the no-bites rule, she started poking her finger in the bottom of each chocolate instead. We won't/can't have chocolates as sweet ever again.

These memories of Morgan are difficult to contemplate. I tend to neutralize the bitterness of such thoughts here. Somehow, writing about memories and feelings that are painful is reliably like removing the splinter or shard of glass from a wound before it festers. As with those excisions, writing about Morgan and our grief is perhaps painful, but for me necessary, and healthy.

There are not enough words, or paper, or keystrokes to help us "get over" this loss; however, I do see a way through, by sharing my feelings to dilute the anguish so that we are able to "get beyond" this agony.

Thank each of you for caring enough to carry us as we move through this rough landscape of life without Morgan Dana Harrington.

241

—⦙⦙⦙—

January 26, 2011   *Anchorage*

On January 26, Dan and I are permitted to visit the field on Anchorage Farm where Morgan's body was found. It's the first anniversary of that discovery. The winding drive up that mountain, the walk through knee-high switchgrass, each step to approach the exact area in that remote, sloping, lonely pasture is weighted with emotion for us. It strikes me: this is our field work.

I crouch down to feel the earth, the ground that held her for 101 days. Of course I wonder if she was alive when he dropped her here. Did she look up at the sky and see stars shining over this field? How much did she suffer?

I remind myself of the anesthesia that shock provides in times of extremis. I have seen this phenomenon many times with patients. Consciousness steps aside, outside of the pain, and provides numbness. I call this anodyne God's grace, and I know he blanketed Morgan with it that night.

It's a quiet place, an unassuming place, this field. My fingertips root down through the tangle of grass and wildflowers. I want to read the braille of the earth itself.

No vestiges of evil remain.

241

—⦙⦙⦙—

The Hunted
4' x 3', oil on canvas
completed 10/6/2011

In response to the upcoming October 17 two-year anniversary of her beloved Virginia Tech student Morgan Dana Harrington's abduction and murder, Jane Lillian Vance has created "The Hunted".

Vance consulted closely with the Harrington family in pursuing her thoughts for this work. They appreciated the thoughtful details of a painting which shows the remote spot on Anchorage Farm where Morgan Harrington's remains were discovered 101 days after her abduction and murder.

"In many ways the painting is beautiful," Vance explains. "Pastoral and quiet. But then your eyes discover the bracelet and the earrings that Morgan was wearing – both which held vigil with her body in that field for three months."

Vance painted an alert deer in the tall grass. "At first you think of the deer as hunted, and with no doubt she is," Vance said. "But I think of that deer as being present that horrible night in a remote field outside Charlottesville. In the painting, she has returned to the scene – to bear witness. We join her – and now, the perpetrators are the hunted."

Vance wrote a piece which she says the painting animates. "This was an emotional painting to create," Vance admitted. "Holding those earrings in the palm of my hand. Seeing my reflection in the gold. Knowing that they held a murderer's reflection. But we are now the ones who pursue. This work shows that we are all looking out, witnessing for justice for the beautiful Morgan Harrington, and are promoting vigilance to help save the next girl."

February 14, 2011   *Woven*

Dearest Morgan, We were there, your Papa and I. We walked to where you were thrown at Anchorage Farm. I needed to see that place just one time, to feel with my hands the earth where the physical stuff of you seeped back into the ground, to see the plants growing on that spot that might be infused with a carbon atom or two from your flesh. I imagine golden hairs from your head woven into the bird nests in the nearby oaks and maples, beautifying, strengthening those homes, as you did ours.

It gives me comfort to think of those elemental parts of you, Morgan, moving forward, combining in new ways, transforming and nourishing new life in that sacred ground on Anchorage Farm.

I am grateful to the land for cradling you, holding you gently as nature dissolved away your tissues and reclaimed the precious molecules of your flesh that a man had destroyed and discarded.

I am grateful that parts of you were accepted and used by other living things. That idea does not erase images of fractured bones, but it does soften the reality somehow.

I am most grateful, Morgan, that the land ultimately returned your body to us so that we could participate in the letting go and through that process attempt to create new growth of our own.

241

We have been supported and loved by so many that it is clearly impossible to respond directly to each of you. Please forgive a group-addressed letter, knowing that it is the only way I can attempt to connect with and update each of you in our extended family.

Dan, Alex, and I have completed our first year without Morgan. There have been difficult patches, but we are finding a way through the landscape of grief. In fact, I am proud to say we have managed to find some forward motion—not just survive.

Dan has been involved in the opening of the Virginia Tech Carilion Medical School (VTC). The inaugural class has almost completed their first school year. This has been a huge project, demanding both insight and fortitude in order to succeed. Dan has managed to shoulder that load and its inherent 12-hour days and come home only to continue working on finding justice for long hours every night. I don't think that I was ever fully aware of his strength and determination until this challenge. He is amazing.

Alex is happy, working as a fashion photo stylist in New York City. His portfolio is impressive: Vogue, W, and I-D. It is remarkable what Alex has accomplished two years post-graduation despite the murder of his beloved sister, Morgan. Alex has a wide group of friends and a great apartment in Brooklyn. We are so proud of him.

I am occupied with many things. Much of our attention and times involves Morgan, such as handling media coverage and promoting the homicide investigation. With excellent leadership from Delegate Eileen Filler-Corn, Dan and I have supported legislation allowing the utilization of familial DNA in Virginia homicides, as well as national funding for missing adult services. Dan and I just returned from presenting at a Law Enforcement Training conference in Wisconsin, a cold place to go in February!

I continue my work with Orphan Medical Network International, OMNI, in Zambia, Africa. I was in Zambia in November for our first graduation ceremony as well as the dedication of our new school building, the Morgan Harrington Educational Wing. In late April, I will make my eighth trip with the OMNI medical team to serve the terribly impoverished inhabitants of the northern Zambian bush. Planning, fundraising, and packing for these annual medical mission trips is a year-long process, but well worth the effort involved.

So you can see that our triangulated family continues to find forward motion to create positive change and legacy to honor Morgan and support each other in the process. It is not easy, but we have been fairly successful in weaving the dark stripe of Morgan's death into the tapestry of our family. The fabric of our lives has certainly changed, but is STILL whole cloth and perhaps beautiful, as well. I believe your prayers and love have made this synthesis and our survival possible. Thank you for holding us up for so long with such caring and strength. You have saved us.

Always,

241
Gil

—⚬⚬—

May 32, 2012   Peonies

My Dearest Mogo,

I have a streaming of thoughts to you constantly, incessantly. Those thought and feelings do not always make it to paper for many reasons. Some of it I know is reluctance to probe the painful places. I think, maybe if I let the feelings alone, pain will dissipate of its own accord. Instead, I find that the emotions fester. I know it is air and light that retards infection and decay – so I will start.

It has been a hard stretch all around. My trip to Africa was both transformative and instructive as it always is, but my absence was particularly difficult for both Dan and Alex this time. Our OMNI team of 15 saw 3077 patients in seven clinics in Zambia. We worked hard and did much good. Our attempt to address the inequities of destiny is gratifying and frustrating as well. I am proud of the many we did help, but heartsick at the throngs we were unable to serve. We will try to do more, be better, smarter, stronger, and more effective – next trip.

The Morgan Harrington Educational Wing is coming along. In the span of a single year, the site has gone from a scrubby field to a building, a big one! With walls and a roof! Some interior work remains, but it is getting close to being completed. So very exciting to watch it grow.

Growth/synthesis/forward motion is imperative to surviving our grief with any kind of wholeness. It is hard to achieve growth and even hard to recognize it when it occurs. I had some insight gardening after my return from Zambia. I was deadheading the spent overblown blossoms of my favorite peonies, and feeling a little sad that I had been absent for the fullness of their flowering. This brought tears when paralleled with the realization I also will miss the full flowering of you, my beloved child.

143

It is incomprehensible that these plants, my peonies, will be back next year – as magnificent and fragrant as ever. I will have another chance to revel in their beauty. You however, will not sprout next year and give us another chance to witness and to love. The Morgan form of you is finished. Over. But here is the very cornerstone of faith to me: the unwavering conviction that the direction of the universe is toward good.

241

In June, 2012, the FBI's graphics team utilizes new computer programming to digitally enhance the 2005 Sketch image from the Fairfax abduction, rape, and attempted murder case, which is forensically linked to Morgan's homicide.

This new graphic is a more human and recognizable composite of Sketch, and the FBI distributes it widely across the East Coast corridor, on highway billboards, and on social media platforms.

Help Save the Next Girl creates a new murdered poster for Morgan, using the new enhanced Sketch face.

James Hetfield with Metallica collaborates with the FBI and features in a new PSA video that shows the digital Sketch image and asks for information and tips. Concern is growing that this serial offender, the Back-to-School Rapist and Killer, will strike again—soon.

July 11, 2012   *Fishlike*

My Dear Morgan,

We have spent several days at the beach. It is so nice to spend time with our beach family, childhood pals and lifetime friends who mourn Morgan's death deeply. Initially, the solitude and the slower tempo are difficult for us. It takes a few more days to turn down the staccato cadence of our lives and follow, instead, the measured rhythm of the ocean. These natural rhythms are healing and calming, but hard to discern when you move so far away from source. It is vital for health to find a slower pace. Many treatment modalities are based on allowing intrinsic patterning to reestablish, like defibrillation for cardiac muscle, or meditation for the spirit. Sometimes, we just have to turn off and reboot the factory settings to function optimally.

That is what we do for ourselves here at the ocean. We defrag the program of our lives by reintroducing the simplicity, strength and beauty of nature into our existence. Funny that it is so hard to give it over to this process. We cling to the distractions and business of our lives like the children playing in the surf cling to inner tubes, thinking that will save them from the force of the tide. It is wrong thinking though. Inner tubes and water wings do help you float in calm water – for a while. Ultimately, what you need to do to survive in water is learn to SWIM. *Be elegant and strong – fishlike in the waves. Morgan, you were like this in the sea. Boldly diving into the pounding waves, your hair silvered like an otter's pelt and your movements as sure and sleek.*

Living requires courage; do not just bob along on the surface, near the shore, afraid. Most of us live below our spiritual capacity. Dad and I have been pushed into deep waters and choose to be brave and to swim; knowing that we are here for a purpose, we choose to show up and try to live at the highest level. This is what I learn from you Morgan – and from the wisdom in these crashing waves.

241

—⚬—

July 24, 2012   Stuck at the big 20: A birthday poem to Mogo

It's another birthday and it ain't too happy
In fact it feels kinda crappy
See, you'll always be
Still Twenty. They tell me you're forever young
And I just have to bite my tongue
Coz from what I can see
Forever young ain't all it's cracked up to be.
Morgan, you were such a beauty
But now you're no way cutie.
I hate to be the one to tell
Honey, you look like Hell.
In two years you've changed a lot.
There was that awkward stage of bones and rot
And now, frankly, don't mean to hurt,
Though forever young, you look old as dirt.
Oh yeah, how dumb,
That's exactly what you have become.
Morgan, you're twenty and holding—your destiny.
Wish instead you were holding me.

241
Mom

—⚬—

Dear Morgan,

We are excited. Alex is coming home for a few days and we are planning to take a short trip together. It is difficult to envision such a thing, a pleasure trip, but we must find new traditions for our triangulated family to survive, to one day thrive again. Contemplating these new travels returns my thoughts to ponderings I had of you at the beach a few weeks ago.

Morgan, there are flashes of you all around. I see your rounded toddler legs pumping up and down the beach. Splashing in the surf and surveying like a little sandpiper. I see your towhead, white in the sunlight like dandelion fluff. I see your skin bronzing and freckles dawning on your nose. I see you dragging surfboards and buckets full of treasured shells over the dunes. I remember the grit of sand-ridden sheets, of course in our bed, introduced by baby feet at nap time snuggle.

I love to think of you grown and sleek in the water, jumping waves for hours with Dad and laughing all the while. I see glimpses of you in other beautiful young girls, Kate, Eva, Iris. I think of you whenever a gesture or turn of phrase reveals youth and promise. These daily little bursts trigger my memory cascade.

Morgan, don't get me wrong, these memories and this process are NOT sad. I actually relish these memories and revisiting our time together. I am so grateful for what we did share. A lifetime, telescoped into 20 short years. Was it your destiny, Morgan? My morning girl, to leave here in the morning of your life? Perhaps.

We are all in the process of becoming. Some of us change more profoundly or more quickly than others. We can only hope to transform into better, more useful stuff. That's the goal. I understand that sometimes this metamorphosis is thrust, indeed forced on us, not chosen. The abrupt onset of transformation makes it harder to discern the innate positive aspects of change. That acceptance follows at a slower pace.

I remember several years ago, pacing at the beach, desperate to find one perfect shell to take to the sickbed of my beloved sister, dying at 50 years old. There were NONE. On this barrier island, pummeled by tides, the shells are all fragments and bits. I wanted perfect—found none.

So I was forced to see a different option. We gathered broken shells, strung them together, and presented Jackie with a mermaid's necklace instead. You have to adapt to circumstances, as difficult as that seems.

Those broken shells are beaten and pounded into bits and become so tiny—grains of sand, which coalesce and become the beach we walk upon. That is what we must do. Take the broken pieces, the shards, the grains and build an island. This synthesis is the key to survival and the very heart of love.

241

Mama

October 11, 2012   *Reluctant*

Morgan you were, and continue to be part of the fabric of our lives. Silly things keep cropping up, like butter. There was always Alex butter (real butter) and Morgan butter (margarine). Now Alex is our only living child and it grieves me a bit to know that this insider Mama knowledge of my family's preference is now irrelevant. Morgan is dead; get over it Gil! I am seeking closure and instead, at time, feel foreclosure – that all our investments of love and nurturing have been forfeited, wasted.

The anguish we feel from Morgan's exclusion from our lives is cutting. The forever-ness of death looms larger now as shock dissipates. We must change this pain into productivity; that is the way to wholeness and healing. I understand the huge opportunities that develop at times of loss. Like a field, you must be plowed; broken open and raw to receive new seeds that can flourish. We are there. We must surrender and let hope germinate. We must let go of attachments to certainty and allow the full spectrum of possibilities to show up. The harvest of that surrender is our very survival.

There is important work yet to be done as a result of Morgan's death; both to honor Morgan and to Save The Next Girl: there is a school in Zambia to continue, a culture of complacency to change, and a medical scholarship to continue funding in Roanoke, and legislation to support that aids law enforcement and protects young women.

I am at best a reluctant activist. I would rather be on my third cup of tea, reading with a dog in my lap, not working, fighting for justice. But this is what I have been given to do and like every task I put my mind to, I will work hard and do my very best.

Morgan, the world was brightened by your time here and will be blessed by your departure as well. I am convinced that divine order exists. Perhaps we will have an arrest in your case only after we have wrung every possible bit of goodness from this terrible wrong. We are trying baby.

241
Mama

—m—

January 26, 2013   *Gristly Anniversary*

When they brought your body back to me
There were just bones to see.
Didn't look like my baby – Morgan D.
No golden hair, no sparkly eyes,
Broken ribs – ugly surprise.
Disposable girl they all said
Skirts too short
Lips're too red
Askin for it they all said
But what you asked for, screamed for, was mercy and release
Know you got no mercy, pray you found some peace
It's so hard to do
This life with no you
Saw your friend at a local place
Saw the message on her face
That she's moved on and we should too
But baby I'm not over the death of you
Gotta shake it off, pity's no use
We've a job to do, still a killer on the loose
It's another anniversary – not the kind you celebrate
But the kind you sorta hate
Even Hallmark passes here, I've looked hard
There's no "Happy we found your daughter's body" card
Morgan, I recon a reckoning is due
Morgan, he'll pay for killing you
And have to atone
For every scream – every moan
For each and every fractured bone

241
Mom

—◠◡◠—

January 9, 2013   *Separating*

My Dearest Morgan,

We have passed the threshold of another Christmas without you. I realize that we have grown stronger from carrying the pain for so long, but it doesn't get easier. Bad days are still fraught with anguish, and good days less desperate, though still flat, sad, and laced with disbelief. I know irrevocably, viscerally, that you are dead but somehow still question this reality. How can it be that you are over? Really?

Morgan, you had such a hard time separating. That first year at Virginia Tech was rough on you. You were such a homebody, so happy to have the foundation of family. I worry now that in some mysterious, instinctive way, you knew somehow that the separation would be the death of you. Should we have listened differently?

The gift of loving and relationship brings with it the vulnerability to loss. It is a risk, but regardless, it is worth us experiencing this pain to have had you as our daughter for twenty years. Morgan, you brought us much joy in your short life. Astoundingly, even years after your murder, your positive legacy continues to reverberate across the world—Zambia, America, Switzerland, and Nepal.

Tragedy can either strengthen or destroy. We choose strength. We embrace the transformation that is not beating us down but forging us into new tools— tools that will hammer and smash the culture of complacency which contributed to your death. We are determined to help save the next girl.

Always,

241
Mama

—∞—

January 26, 2013   *Third Anniversary*

Standing again on the Copley Bridge, I spoke these words to the Charlottesville Community:

Morgan was found three years ago today, on Anchorage Farm, by happenstance, seeming sheer luck.

We haven't had much luck since.

It's time. Our turn. Morgan's unsolved homicide needs a hero.

To you who are sheltering Sketch, I ask you to be that hero. It's time, past time, to do the right thing. Act from your compassion and call Virginia State Police with your information. Act, and help us save the next girl.

It has been 1,196 days since he killed our Morgan. That's a lot of days robbed from Morgan, from our family. It's 1,196 days that Sketch has been free and able to do whatever he likes, and what he likes to do is rape and murder women. I bet he has already picked out the next body dumpsite, and is starting to scout for the next girl.

Please, I beg of you, stop him. Before he does it again. We need your help.

241

—◊◊—

February 2, 2013   *Bound by Gravity*

Dearest Morgan,

Sorry to be despondent, but this bleak grey month of February has nested in like a boulder, cold, hard, and immobile. I am struggling. Yearning for release from our challenging reality, but bound.

I am tied to the world by obligation: to you and your legacy, to solving your brutal murder, to holding up Dan and Alex through this obscene desecration. Bound here by frantic canine scratching at the door, brown eyes at the food bowl, bushels of dirty laundry cascading like yeasted dough from the hamper. These implied promises hold me fast. I am at core a doer, a worker. I cannot turn aside when duty calls.

It is tempting, though. It would be so easy to let go, to float away. Is this the ultimate power of gravity/sorrow? It holds us here with tethers of love and obligation. Would that the strands might fray, separate, perhaps release, because the tie so often chafes.

We need some magic here, Morgan. An arrest would mean a rest. Bring it on. Please.

Always, 241
Mama

—◊◊—

March 23, 2013   *Three and a half*

Dear Morgan,

The bad times are laced with anguish and pain, the good times filled with disbelief—still. It is three and a half years since you were murdered and it's still hard to fathom. The wellspring of your great potential lost. Writing this, Morgan, I find myself punching down hard on the computer keys, like a typewriter, as if stroke force will prevent your erasure from the world. How can you be over? How can we shoulder this burden for the rest of our days? But we must. Really, there is no other choice. We must relinquish control and old expectations—over, and over, and over—and somehow face a new reality, head on.

Our daily landscape is still a minefield riddled with objects/thoughts/ words that unleash memories which quickly plunge into emotions and grief. Photos displayed around the house that used to comfort now sometimes lash. I catch sight of your beautiful face and smile and quickly try to shake off the horrific mental hologram that seeks to superimpose images of your gap-toothed skull. I look at a picture on the fridge and stop myself from the gruesome calendar math inherent in an image. I try not to calculate how many days you had left to live in each and every scene.

We have grown some of the muscles that surviving loss demands. We navigate the tough places and hold feelings in check. Just when I think I have successfully walled off the no longer possible life, I see Dan weeping over wedding dressings shown on TV. Not our path now. So much anticipated joy surrendered. On Easter, there will be no Peeps here. A ridiculous and silly thing to miss, I know, but it is another little whiff of fun we have had to dismiss. Morgan, you thought that Peeps were hilarious: the Easter equivalent of fruitcake, always present and yet never consumed. And so they were a funny inclusion in every Easter basket I ever assembled—another task that is no longer mine to do.

I am grateful that it is easier to hold these feelings in check than it was years ago. Morgan, our life is not so sharp and fraught with pain. We are making it. Feels sort of like we have moved from walking on shards of glass to merely walking on eggshells. Still a tricky path to navigate and one I wish we didn't have to walk. We miss you always and mourn the loss of joy.

241
Mama

.

—ᘉ—

May 5, 2013   *Lumber*

Dear Morgan,

Scrap lumber, that's what it really is, a pine board about 7 feet tall and two inches wide, with a hole drilled in the top. Your grandfather made it. Actually, he made two of them, one for each of you kids right after you were born—your special "grow sticks." Poppy made the grow sticks so that the sprint of time couldn't erase the dramatic changes that babies undergo to become adults. Rather than inscribe a door frame with ascending hatch marks to note your increasing height, you always had your grow stick hanging in the bedroom to record that progression. All three bedrooms: the first, in Charlottesville, that you shared with Alex when we brought you home from the hospital. Your second bedroom was here in Roanoke—a small room, but big enough for your crib—and the room you insisted on later because it was next to your big brother, Allie. You took possession of your third and final bedroom as a middle schooler when you moved across the hall to a more spacious room that would better accommodate sleepovers and loud music. Your grow stick was installed next to the closet and you kept growing and recording the miraculous transformations life brings.

It is infinitely precious for me to translate the scratchy marks you made on the board next to the closet. Naturally the top mark is Dan, tall papa, rock of our family. I remember each and every notation on the wood. How excited you were when you were 'officially' taller than me—March, 2001—when you were 12. As a little girl you were amazed to see the mark that showed "how big I was when I got borned," July 24, 1989—19.5 inches long. The lowest marks near the ground are really hilarious, where you kept the pet record. I smile to see that our little kitten Zeb was seven inches tall on 9/92. I recall the difficulty of your 3-year-old self, taking that measurement, though it was not nearly as hard as making your parakeet Opal sit still long enough to be recorded on 4/99.

For the record, Morgan, your murderer shrunk you to a dimension of 10 x 10 x 4 inches, the size of a cigar box where you now reside.

Memories permeate the marks you inscribe in the wood grain of your grow stick. Contemplating it is bittersweet but the sadness is tolerable because we had much fun with the silliness of the task. What is still excruciating beyond bearing is the flip side of the board. That's where you planned to chart the growth of your own children, your anticipated family, those beloveds who will never exist and who were also stolen from us. The unmarked and forever empty expanse of wood on the flip side is invisibly inscribed with pain, a virtual Rosetta Stone of loss.

In the midst of continuing agony, Morgan, your family keeps choosing strength. We choose survival. We choose love. We continue to choose, insist upon, and embrace growth.

241

—◊—

June 27, 2013   *Waves*

Dearest Mogo,

Papa and I are with the crew at the beach. It is particularly hard on Dan to be here without you as the special wave-jumping water buddy. This was always a magical time of bonding for you and Papa. Laughing and splashing in the surf; both gleeful and childlike in those shared salty, sandy moments. So fleeting – that joy. The membrane to earlier times and to the magnitude of our loss is more permeable in this place. We feel the empty space more; even seek it out; like you search the arch of the mandible with your tongue probing vacant space for the missing tooth.

Morgan we miss you like crazy; always will, but we are trying so hard to create something positive and grow, even in our sorrow. The gash, the wound has begun to granulate but the protection of scar has not yet formed. We still feel pretty raw much of the time. Folks say, "I don't know how you can survive this!" Well here it is, my insight on how to cope with catastrophic loss: "I'll have my breakdown just as soon as I get this load of towels out of the dryer – repeat as necessary".

Morgan, so we soldier on, holding fast to the belief; like you clung tightly to your float in this turbulent North Carolina Ocean, that the sorrow and pain of loss is mitigated by the promise of rebirth and transformation. The inevitable and ever malignant death is actually the means which allows spirit to rise. We are open to transformation, knowing that love abides.

241
Mama

—◊—

July 4, 2013   *Paparazzi*

Avon, NC

Dearest Morgan,

We are gathered here at the Avon beach again – Dan's 32nd trip with the same group of friends to these shores. I joined in a bit later, you and Alex later still – first as unsteady toddlers, squealing in the surf and eating fistfuls of sand. I think you loved both the salt and the crunch of it.

As a 7-year-old you adamantly dragged your own "surfboard" float up to the boardwalk and stairs to the ocean. Your skin slowly bronzing, a spray of tiny freckles on your nose, hair white blonde from the sun, strands blowing in the wind like an areola of light. The light was called to you – golden child.

Later you were awkward teens; uneasy in morphing bodies, changing roles. Only here the relentless winds and tides blew away pretense and helped you to find/be yourself in this stark simple place. It was a wondrous and healing process to watch.

That last summer was the best of all – you were so gloriously alive and joy-filled, radiantly beautiful. Happiness beaming from you, like a Kleig light. Dan in particular was blessed with the pleasure of spending beach time with an accomplished grown-up daughter. You two "grown-ups" cavorted and splashed and played together like children in the waves. Thank you for these precious moments.

This is our fourth trip to Avon, North Carolina, since your murder. It's getting better. We are getting better at feeling the loss, the pain and letting it pass, flow through us like a wave, feeling and not resisting the destructive power which allows us to remain standing in our high tide of grief.

We are figuring it out but it is slow going. Morgan do you remember the scads of pictures I always took – a mama paparazzi, anxious to record every family moment for posterity; I don't take pictures at the beach anymore; I just can't find the family.

241
Mama

—⚡—

July 10, 2013   *Grains*

I am still pondering the ocean.

Fate has delivered us an immutable roadblock. I can sit here for the rest of my days and stew over why I cannot have the life I had anticipated, or I can detour and find a new way, even prosper by so doing. It is a choice; switch of perspective. You can feel like a "whack a mole game" or you can decide to feel like a blade that is being honed to strike for good.

Morgan, your death has caused me to strengthen my spiritual struts, to reaffirm my thoughts and cognition. This hideous murder has forced us to change. We attempt to use the loss and pain to break through and awaken. I am learning how to deal with this sad, messy, unsanitized life. How to love it all. That is the difficult but necessary response.

Relinquish old expectations, secure in the belief that love always shows up. Pain can serve as a vehicle that allows for love's transformation. I see the lesson in the sandy beach of the Outer Banks. The beautiful sand and undulating dunes are actually a compilation of massive destruction. So many individual shells pummeled and pounded until at some point they no longer resemble conch, clam, or scallop but leave behind a singular identity and become beach. A mysterious process as redemption follows demolition. I accept the lesson, even in the face of the ultimate challenge of your hideous death, Morgan. Life, growth and love are coming around again.

241
Love, Mama

—ɯ—

August 27, 2013   *Back to school, again*

Morgan, my sweet girl, I am not loving the mall just now; see, it's "back to school" time again. Remember "back to school", back before you were dead?

It is a time of new beginnings, and hope, and a passel of jitters thrown in besides. Back to school shopping for the perfect binder; reams of papers, fistfuls of sharpies and pens. You loved to put your binder together and make a plan to attack the new academic year. Remember the flurry of heavy telephone conferences to discuss and debate with all your friends "What to wear the first day? Is it ok to pack your lunch or does that look nerdy? Maybe it is better to buy from the cafeteria? Did you get the "good" math teacher? Where in heck are all the different classrooms?"

Lockers – that was a big stressor when you entered middle school. Could you manage to work the combination lock? We even went covertly to the school building a couple of days before class started (very nerdy) with WD-40 to grease up the lock. We practiced and practiced your combination until the lock sprang open in your palm effortlessly.

Morgan, you were always both anxious and thrilled to start classes again in the Fall. You loved all the possibilities and promise of a new beginning that back to school implied. Tragically, all over for us now, no promise, no hope, no beginning, just your end. That's why I have to stay away from the mall for a bit.

241
Mama

—∞—

September 18, 2013   Scientific

Autopsy Report

Which seat do you choose? Among all the comfortable chairs in this house, which one is the right one to support me as I open and read the Medical Examiner's autopsy report for our slain daughter, Morgan Dana Harrington?

It is a thick envelope. The kids always said a fat envelope was a good sign; typically meaning something positive, like an acceptance to college. Thick or pancake flat envelope makes no difference in this missive; it is all bad news. It is stupid of me to be so avoidant of this written document. I have seen the damage, felt the bones, smelled the rot. Still, to experience the objectivity and scientific analysis inherent in the autopsy report is so disturbing. She wasn't a 20 year old white female, 5 feet 7 inches.... She was Morgan, our baby girl with shiny hair, flashing eyes and such sweet silky soft skin. How could he have ended all that? I will never understand the evil, the cruelty of this killer.

He ripped your ribs from their cage; he did a two-handed twist on your upper arm and spiral-shattered your living bone; he knocked out your front teeth; he fractured your skull. And he left his dog's hair all over your shirt.

As time passes, Morgan, I feel mounting urgency about other young women who may fall in this predator's path. I feel his blood lust growing and am frantic in my determination to Help Save the Next Girl.

159

Morgan, your papa and I are tired but remain steadfast in our search for your killer. We work diligently also to change the culture of complacency and complicity that accepts violence against young women as status quo or incidental occurrences. That indifference must be shifted. I refuse to accept the false premise that these lives don't matter. You surely did.

241
Love Mama

———⚛———

October 25, 2013   *Flags*

Dear Mogo,

We are all taking on a bit of water just now. I am not exactly sure why. I think it has something to do with the time of year. This is the season when you were killed. It is also the start of school and all the promise that youth entails is on display at every corner, waiting for the school bus – or tiptoeing into the campus bookstore agog at new horizons. Those vistas are closed to us now as we try to live an inexplicable life.

I went to Charlottesville yesterday. Just couldn't stop myself. I had to advise caution and awareness to a new crop of kids in that place where a predator still walks free. I know students feel invincible, Teflon coated, but while a murderer roams they are in actuality – fresh meat, fodder. It is too late to save you my darling, but having felt this anguish, I can't quit on the next girl.

That's what my trip was about: **Help Save the Next Girl.** *I will not let your murder fade to beige and be swept aside – as suits so many. Towards that end, I went back to the bridge of your abduction. I weeded the boxwood plant and anointed its feet with iridescent glass jewels that catch the sunlight and spit it back like fire. I festooned the gray granite of your marker with multicolored prayer flags that gesture blessings into every breeze. It may be for naught, silly even, for I know they clear away these expressions soon after I leave, but my urge to adorn and make note of sacred ground is a mother's right, in fact a mother's duty. Mine to perform – and so I shall.*

Still I find it hard to believe that you are over, finito. How can that be? Morgan, you were so big. You drew in all the light and banged it back, amped up x 10! So full of energy and life and fun! Now husks of bone and ash. What reality is this? Not the one I choose – but the reciprocal reality is madness.

Though I dabble there at times, it frightens and holds little comfort. Pity, or I might take up residence in that space of altered mind where I could conjure you at will.

Morgan, I miss you so.

Always,
241
Mom

—⚓—

December 11, 2013   *Bags, Boxes*

Our path through the holidays: closed Christmas boxes

We realized soon after Morgan's murder that holidays would be tricky ground to navigate for our shrunken/triangulated family. Old traditions had to be jettisoned, too painful, and new traditions had to be developed.

Our new Christmas traditions involve many firmly closed Christmas boxes. Some of those boxes are memory boxes that we force the lid on to prevent self-injury. Like: I won't think about the elaborate Christmas rituals that Morgan and Alex invented as children. They not only put out cookies and milk for Santa, but also placed carrots on the front lawn for his reindeer. Dan didn't mind standing in for Santa and munching the cookies, but honestly I know Dan didn't love searching the yard with flash lights Christmas Eve to locate and nibble the reindeer's carrots. Nope, won't open that box.

Some of our closed Christmas boxes are actual boxes – like the box of ornaments in the basement. I can't bear to see all the kid-crafted decorations, though one in particular keeps popping into my head. Probably in 2nd or 3rd grade, Morgan came home proudly presenting the ornament she had made in class. It was actually sort of hideous. A flattened pop can sprayed with gold and given a shake of glitter as adornment. Every year thereafter I tried to position the darn thing on the very back of the tree to hide its garish awfulness. Inevitably Morgan would seek it out and place it front and center on the tree for all to admire. Definitely must keep the lid on the ornament box.

In fact we don't even fill Christmas boxes with presents anymore. I use bags instead now. See, I am a hasty/sloppy present wrapper. Morgan took over that task long ago and loved to tie each bow precisely and decorate all the packages like works of art. I just cannot replay that scene. So now all gifts are placed in bags. Another shift in tradition that allows us to skate through this emotionally charged time of year.

I have to think that Morgan, our beautiful shiny out of the box girl, helps us somehow traverse these rough stretches. We are not unscathed by the holidays. Predictably we become a little raw around the edges. Yes, raw, diminished but still whole and moving forward. Raw, but still permeable to the joy of this season of giving. Raw, but so grateful for the time we had with Morgan, our precious little girl now placed in yet another closed box.

241

—⁓—

December 15, 2013   *Wobble*

I am not proud of this one. But in the interest of transparency and truth-telling, I feel I must share the darkness that devastation casts.

Sometimes, I just want to weep. For all of us. For our pain. For the pain you felt, Morgan, as you were destroyed. The loss is so much to carry.

We have worked so hard and we are tired. When we are most exhausted, when we recoil at the vertigo of being on the edge of emotional despair in perpetuity, when we consider we have no sure end to our struggle, our vulnerability allows self-defeating thoughts to trickle in. Then, the world grows dark.

The truth is, Morgan, that every day, every single day since you were killed, I have had some moments of total despair. I lose the mindful surrender I work hard to find, and I totally reject the reality of our lives.

How could this hideous murder have happened to you? To us? Why? Why? And why can't they find and stop him?

It's not unusual for me to be driving somewhere, like maybe over a bridge, and I start to fantasize: I could just drive off into nothingness, oblivion, opt out. It seems tempting, no more pain.

But then there is the mountain of obligation, beginning with a small dog, who is waiting at home for food, water, and a walk; Dan, as shattered as I am, who needs solace, not more agony; and Alex, your brother, still so raw and wounded from this murder.

An elaborate group structure of caring, duty, and accountability holds me fast. I know how selfish and stupid it is to consider opting out. I remember, Morgan, how hard you fought for every moment of life, for every breath.

I am ashamed of these episodes of weakness and tiredness, Morgan. I promise I will continue searching for Justice. Surely, someday, there must be an answer.

Surely, finding and stopping your killer will hold our redemption.

241

—⁂—

December 20, 2013   *Soapsuds and Wormholes*

Trap doors that spring open and hurl you full on into the pain of loss are hidden cleverly. Camouflaged so subtlety that you don't recognize the danger until it's too late to take evasive action. Protect yourself, head down, Brace, Brace, Brace, here it comes – again.

Couldn't find my usual laundry detergent at the store last week. What to do? I am a creature of habit, reluctant to switch brands, but overflowing laundry bins prompted a change. I bought another product. Easy, right? No problem, until I did a load of clothes today.

The new soap's scent hung in the damp air and permeated the laundry. And it was the exact smell and steamy feel as Jackie's cellar laundry room in Zurich. Dead now for 9 years, but that smell sucked me into a wormhole back to a past when we were both young mothers with mountains of laundry to wash together. A time when we cooked gallons of macaroni and cheese, and PB & Jelly (cut only on the diagonal), and pancakes with faces. A busy time. We worked hard and had much fun in the process. The clean soapy smell triggered such a strong memory that I could almost feel the texture and gesture of folding warm towels together in your home with Anna and Eva underfoot. Nine years ago my sister, Kena, before you were whittled away into nothingness by savage gastric cancer. Dead at 51. Back when there were 4 cousins at play together.

Though bittersweet, I cherish this olfactory memory link to my dear sister Jackie. I would love to conjure Morgan in such a meaningful sensory way also. Too bad that Morgan, stolen from us at 20 years old, was too young to have done so many of life's tasks, like choosing a brand of laundry soap.

241

—⁂—

April 15, 2014   *Sufferin Stew – A Recipe for Survival*

Take a large portion of tough meat cut it to the bone
1 bunch rough organic stuff
Cover with an ocean of sorrow
Add 1 lump faith
Bring to a hard boil
Let simmer a long while, steeping in its own juices
Just a pinch of grace and everything softens and melds together
It'll slide down real easy
Serve warm
It ain't no roast, but it will sustain, nurture, bless
Please take your place, wait in line
Portions always plentiful and fine
No need to push or be loud
Lots of sufferin around to feed the crowd.

241

—⚬—

June 16, 2014   *Band of Gold*

Dear Morgan

We know now that we will survive, but still have to figure out how to actually live and flourish post you. The means is literally at hand. I got your gold signet ring back from the Virginia State Police recently. We all have the same ring and choose to wear this family emblem frequently. I am finding myself changed by wearing your ring. My immediate response to it has surprised me a bit. It/you elevates me throughout my day.

I see the flash of gold on my hand as I rinse out a tea cup and I pray "please Morgan, help me see things more clearly." I smile to realize that I now pray to you rather than for you, knowing you are beyond all pain and harm, - angelic now. Reading in my spot on the couch I turn a page and fee the unaccustomed weight of your ring. I am reminded to give thanks for this day, for the sweet, light pressure of Kirby's doggy chin on my leg. Blessing.

Wearing your ring, the one you were wearing when you were beaten, and your heart stopped beating, is my sacred honor and duty. The beauty of it, the pain of it continues to open me and whisper its teaching. I promise to listen so carefully and to stop grasping worry and fear and constructing barriers to wisdom. Hoping that acceptance and understanding will arrive eventually, I hear, learn, and choose to let the negative slip aside and instead allow growth to have its way – untethered.

Always and always,

241
Mama

—⚏—

July 15, 2014   *No mo doe – or Mogo*

I have observed with curiosity and horra
what results when deer meets car-a
she was hit at high speed
left on the road side to suffer and bleed

and in 2 weeks there's hardly a trace
weather and scavengers help to erase
this dying place
only a few ribs and vertebrae
left for them to clear away

the doe was beauty personified
soft flanked, big eyed
grace immense
effortless she cleared the fence
to meet her fate
on the car's grate

tragic destiny – but accident
Morgan, I hate that your life was taken with intent
and your body also tossed away
to decompose and decay

your story Mogo
quite different from the doe
not accident with S.U.V.
but murder by S.O.B.
took you from me

our baby
how can it be?

241
Mama

—⚡—

August 12, 2014   *Mogo memory medley*

You were missing but not by choice
Had to call your cell phone, just to hear your voice
And you'd say, "I'll get back to you as fast as I can"
But you never came back to me and Dan
Funny to remember the little girls who'd say
"I'm gonna be famous someday"
I'd smile and shake my head
But just as soon as you were dead
Honey, you were so right
One cold October night
After a brief and violent fight
You became front-page news
Such a strange place to be
Your face staring back from our TV
We carry the numbers of the State Police
Phone rings and there is no peace
Guys with tripods traipse through the halls
Our life's become a free for all
I plea on camera for your release
Said, Come home, Morgan, please
Now find you only in my dreams
The heart still screams
No way
No how
We still need our baby now

241
166   *Mama*

Recovery and Justice

Part III

At the beginning of September, 2014, we have spent five years reflecting on the nature of evil. My heart will probably always ask: what is the genesis of evil? When does opportunism pass the line and become evil? Are you evil from birth, from the very beginning?

Or does evil mature and transform like flower buds? They start out green and tiny. They slowly ripen, and become colored. They change, and become a different thing. There are still vestiges of a bud in the flower, but the flower is a whole new thing.

I wish we had a sensitive device, or a test, to warn us when a human crosses the line from opportunism into evil. I know Morgan's killer would scream the danger alarm off the chart.

I will always know that Morgan really did have it all, brains, beauty, loving family, friends. And everything in her life was in order: she had found her passion and chosen a career, made a home, learned to cook (scrambled eggs anyway), had a passport, ready to travel, vaccines up-to-date. Just bursting with potential, but Morgan, you expired before your driver's license will in 2017.

The only thing you lacked was time, precious time. Such a short life. You were only 20 years old when he killed you. Your time ran out. Such a damn shame. What a waste.

What vile thing came to the Copely Bridge? It was a rainy night and cold, when he slaughtered you and dumped your body like a field-dressed doe onto the sodden matted grass and dirt at Anchorage farm.

The bloodlust of a dangerous predator still bewilders me. I just cannot comprehend the desire to hurt and maim. But evil does exist. I know, and he murdered you.

We are getting tired, need a break. At times we long to tuck tail and slink away. But there is a killer out there whose appetite only increases. His jets are starting to hum. His compulsions grow. Is it time?

Morgan, Music Fan

Our girl wanted to go out and dance
Didn't know she took such a chance
Just wanted to be part of the scene
Didn't know people could be so damned mean
That anyone would want to hurt her
He was checking the scene, planning a murder
Evil lurking on the periphery
To kill and vanquish her beauty
Evil like killed Lennon, King, JFK
Decided to take out a girl that day
And threw her like refuse in a field of hay
Now I have felt the heft of her skull in my palm
An abomination for any Mom
Your crime and your evil fill me with rage
We will not rest til you're locked in a cage
We will catch you, I know that we can
We're after you, me and Dan
So other girls will be safe on the street
To follow the music
To follow the beat

241

Is it time? It is, if he gets a chance, finds the weak one, and seizes the opportunity. I continue to beg Charlottesville, don't let that happen. Don't let him kill again. Be vigilant. Be aware. Participate in your community, know your neighbors. Look out for one another. Please, help save the next girl.

Faith is a raft that will help you move through the flume of rough water.

Faith is not a tight door that will keep the force and depth of sorrow out.

Spirit, like water, flows and will find its way. I believe that God is present in all things, and that present in every situation is the opportunity for good. Light will always return from some horizon to dispel the darkness. Spirit will always lead to greater good. I am convinced of that positive direction, led by that belief in relief and regeneration.

Though I am firmly grounded in my belief that the world is inherently good, undeniably, sorrow still swells the calm. Loss is inevitable. In response, I believe our choice is to disintegrate and collapse, or to grow and move forward.

Sorrow is like a dog who lives in your house. The dog spirals to nest in an old familiar spot, crosses its paws, sighs, and sleeps. But the next day, sorrow wakes in your home, and it circles and settles again, and it will do, every new day. It's your dog.

We have our terrible injury. We are sorrowful, our family, accompanied always by sorrow. But we have moved out from the raw anguished grief over Morgan's death, into a gentler place of mourning.

How did we get to this easier place, given that we have experienced grief beyond the normal lot?

I can understand that many who experience catastrophic loss never manage to reach this place. Our family's equation for survival is this:

LOVE ↓ PAIN

LOVE = SERVICE

SERVICE = The recovery engine to wholeness and repair

↑ SERVICE → ↑ ACCEPTANCE

↑ ACCEPTANCE → ↓ AGONY

↓ AGONY → ↑ PEACE

With peace, you can reboot to your birthright, your factory settings of joy. And p.s., ACCEPTANCE does NOT = SURRENDER.

Our family is smaller now. But I know each of us has grown because of the tragic murder of our Morgan. I believe that the effort of struggle strengthens us.

Our exceptional challenges require and demand exceptional responses. We will soldier on, knowing that we are always given the tools to succeed in every challenge. This is the cornerstone of my faith. The trick is to recognize and use those tools correctly.

Spirit becomes most evident when life cannot be managed. I repeat to myself: at the point of snap, you can break, Gil, or choose to transform. That dark place and those sharp times can generate a fragile surrender, and with acceptance, solace comes.

The biggest barrier is mental. When we are broken, the fracture place can become the strongest. Loss is unavoidable. The assimilation of suffering is a necessary life skill. To find meaning in pain transforms suffering into a tool for growth.

Thank God, we can look back now and see growth.

Typically Dan and I used to be pretty private and apolitical individuals, not apathetic, just busy balancing work and family. Morgan's murder changed that.

We have been determined to use every possible tool to help us find the monster who killed our daughter. We began to research and support legislation that we believed would enhance safety.

Dan became interested in the forensic use of familial DNA by law enforcement. As he began to scrutinize laws and cases, Dan observed that only three states use this laboratory assay forensically. Dan spoke to the General Assembly, legislators heard the issue with new awareness, and subsequently, familial DNA legislation was signed into law in the Commonwealth of Virginia.

In recent years, Dan and I have testified in Richmond, in support of several other bills that are passed. That legislation includes expansion of DNA databanks to require submission of DNA for first-degree misdemeanor convictions, HB 1617. We were also grateful to support the excellent leadership of Virginia Delegate Eileen Filler-Corn's HB 1785, which requires external reporting of sexual assaults on Virginia college campuses.

This role of activism for us was unexpected and vitally important. I am proud of this political engagement's implication for thousands of families. Our daughter's legacy now includes these new legal tools. If any one of these three laws we fought for had been in place in 2009, Morgan Harrington would still be alive today.

Morgan worked at the Virginia Tech Carilion School of Medicine, VTC, during the summer before she was killed. It was a transformative time for Morgan.

MORGAN DANA HARRINGTON SCHOLARSHIP

The experience of working with her father and so many professional role models made Morgan decide to become an educator herself. That was the service she would provide to the world.

The Morgan Dana Harrington Memorial Scholarship Fund at the Virginia Tech Carilion School of Medicine was established when Morgan's remains were found. This scholarship tribute was announced by Dan at her funeral. The scholarship is designed to help VTC medical students defray some of the cost of their education and is awarded now on a need basis to two students every year.

Funding comes from donations and several other sources. The "Docs for Morgan" basketball game is the brainchild of Dr. Tracey Criss, a dear family friend, and it quickly became an annual event. The "Docs for Morgan" game pits medical students against their medical faculty and is the source of much fun, camaraderie, funding, and healing.

Imagine how it feels for Dan, when cheerleaders have assembled from different Help Save the Next Girl chapters' schools, and so many of his colleagues and the students who look up to Dr. Harrington, all of them dressed in differently colored Help Save the Next Girl shirts, are joined by local television anchors emceeing the game, everyone gathered and playing as a tribute to Morgan.

We love the circularity of the "Docs for Morgan" effort. In response to injury—Morgan's murder--the community supports and contributes to the education of medical students, who in turn will contribute to the health and well-being of community. Nice.

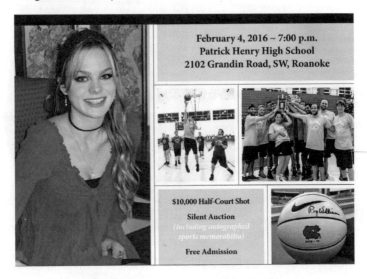

February 4, 2016 ~ 7:00 p.m.
Patrick Henry High School
2102 Grandin Road, SW, Roanoke

$10,000 Half-Court Shot

Silent Auction
(including autographed sports memorabilia)

Free Admission

DOCS FOR MORGAN
BASKETBALL CHALLENGE 2016

Virginia Tech Carilion School of Medicine students will try to defend their title against a team of Jefferson College of Health Sciences students and Carilion Clinic residents and attendings.

ABOUT MORGAN

Morgan Harrington interned at the Virginia Tech Carilion School of Medicine the summer before her death. In her short time there, her kind heart, ebullient laugh, and can-do spirit left an indelible imprint on the school.

DOCS FOR MORGAN

Docs for Morgan was formed in 2012 by Carilion Clinic physicians who wanted to honor Morgan and support her parents, Dr. Daniel Harrington and Mrs. Gil Harrington. The group has since expanded to include other friends and supporters.

THE SCHOLARSHIP

This fundraiser—the fourth annual Docs for Morgan basketball challenge—supports the Morgan Dana Harrington Memorial Scholarship Fund at the Virginia Tech Carilion School of Medicine. The scholarship honors Morgan's passion for education.

To learn more, visit tinyurl.com/docsbasketball2016, or email lpearobaker@carilionclinic.org

With unexpected generosity, Metallica also continues to direct all proceeds from Enter Sandman/Jump T-shirts sold at Virginia Tech to Morgan's scholarship.

We are immensely grateful. Our family has lost so much, but we have received an outpouring of love in equal measure. That outpouring has been instrumental to our healing. It is fitting that this tsunami of kindness has been directed to producing medical healers who will serve in our communities. This resupply of medicine and compassion in the world is how you combat evil.

We find a great deal of comfort from the positive legacy we have created in Morgan's honor. The Morgan Harrington Educational Wing at OMNI Village in Zambia continues to graduate students who qualify for further education. These accomplished students will go on to become leaders in their community, and stakeholders in the new, enfranchised Africa.

Simultaneously, the Morgan Harrington Memorial Scholarship at Virginia Tech Carilion School of Medicine has so far been able to make distribution to four doctors-in-training.

Help Save the Next Girl has grown and really changed the culture of complacency that surrounds predatory violence.

Dan and I are determined to save the next girl and believe that is best accomplished through education on campuses and in public and private schools. The founding chapter of Help Save the Next Girl began at Morgan's school, Virginia Tech. Ian Heflin, Morgan's friend and classmate in the last Spring of her life, remembers: he sat just to Morgan's left, in McBryde Hall, classroom 219. He began the first club and puts to use his abilities with graphics and computers, resulting in a compelling online platform for VT Help Save the Next Girl. Iconic Virginia Tech football coach Frank Beamer endorses Help Save the Next Girl, producing inspiring public service announcements. He cries, accepting a print of *The Hunted*. Other schools continue to join the movement and open across the Commonwealth and beyond. We are really getting the message of safety awareness out to young people.

Early on, Help Save the Next Girl incorporated and obtained 501(3)(C) designation. Our dear friend Bruce Bryan, who serves on the Board, used his media savvy to extend our reach. Bruce shepherded online web ads, radio spots, and helped orchestrate our national public service announcement.

Our 31-second public service announcement won admiration and awards. We shot it locally. Friends' daughters and young women, many of them students from Virginia Tech's Help Save the Next Girl chapter, gathered in a field on a gentle mountaintop to stand together and recite the Help Save the Next Girl pledge.

One of those students was Annalee Marshall, slated to become the next president of VT HSTNG. Only 20, like Morgan, Annalee died in a Christmas day car accident. Her family still sees her beautiful silhouette and hears her voice whenever our public service announcement plays on television or radio, proud to remember Annalee's passion and commitment to help save the next girl.

We will not become a statistic.
We will Help Save The Next Girl.

X_____

This creative collaborative energy and barrage of positive messages is how you change the culture of complacency that has surrounded predatory violence against young women. You saturate the environment, including conversations and media, using every tool at your disposal, with the message that not one of our daughters is a disposable commodity. Not one. They matter. And you had better believe we care. Big time.

Help Save the Next Girl holds countless events over the years since we formed, vigils, rallies, talks, information sessions. Our finances and our tools are humble and modest. We use chalk, ribbons, candles, buttons, plastic bracelets, a series of t-shirts in different colors and designs, even Lifesaver candies as means to raze the wall of indifference that surrounds predatory violence. But our determination is profound.

We continue bringing energy and awareness to unsolved missing and homicide cases in our region. Shockingly, there continue to be so many of them, a dizzying number of absent beloveds.

Before Morgan's remains were found, Amanda St. Clair, Help Save the Next Girl champion and on-line wizard, began charting unsolved homicides and missing cases in Virginia.

The obscene scatter of loss graphically revealed by the map looks like a Center for Disease Control emergency outbreak study. The pattern is not simply a bizarre local cluster phenomenon. We see a cultural epidemic.

In response, we create safety materials, booklets pitched to Brownie Scouts, flyers, missing posters, and disseminate them widely, to media and to law enforcement, electronically and hand-to-hand. I believe we have helped to awaken our community, our state to the reality of burgeoning predatory dangers.

We caution: predators do exist, in every community.

Nice places, like Charlottesville, Lovingston, and Blacksburg. And evil comes in all shapes and sizes. Sometimes it's hulking and dressed in a cold scowl like Sketch. Sometimes it wears a skinny Golem disguise like convicted murderer, Randy Allen Taylor. It can wear every possible shape, size, and color.

Despite all efforts at prevention, when the worst happens, predatory violence has tremendous reverberations. After the victim is struck, then the damage extends and fractures families, and continues even more widely, to erode other relationships and communities.

But you can make an extraordinary choice. At the very second an injury is over, healing can commence.

You must allow and encourage the healing, but it can begin immediately.

Dan and I have come to see that community really is the best medicine for grief. An aroused community is a determined engine of compassion, kindness, casseroles, and deep spiritual healing.

The Help Save the Next Girl Facebook page now has 53,000 participants and there are fifty school-based Help Save the Next Girl chapters. Young people are reading our pledge, and talking again about their part in proactive social responsibility.

Our group also works hard to bring awareness to recent missing cases and unsolved homicides in our area. There have been a heartbreaking number of those cases just in central Virginia, including Bethany Decker, Bonnie Santiago, Cassandra Morton, Samantha Clark, Sage Smith, and Alexis Murphy… Each instance of a missing person opens a painful abscess in our communities. Every abduction scathes not only a family, but, like Agent Orange, burns the fabric of who we all are.

In September, 2014, we hear the gut-wrenching news that there is yet another.

A vibrant, athletic, smart coed is missing from Charlottesville. She is 18 years old, and has just begun enjoying her second year at the University of Virginia.

Her name is Hannah Graham.

We go into high gear.

Once you have membership in this ugly club, the families of the missing or murdered, you will move heaven and earth to help save the next girl.

Help Save the Next Girl holds vigils across the state for Hannah, which news stations live-stream. We beseech the community of Charlottesville for information. We support the robust effort that Chief Tim Longo and his Charlottesville Police initiate, and initiate fast.

The semaphore of ribbons that festoon the Copley Bridge, white for RG, pink for Alexis, purple for Morgan, now includes a bright orange ribbon, waving with the other girls'. Hannah's favorite color.

Video surveillance from Charlottesville's downtown pedestrian mall ultimately reveals a suspect in Hannah's disappearance.

His name is Jesse Matthew.

The next few days are bizarre, high octane beyond description. There is an abduction with the intent to defile charge, an escape, an arrest, and an extradition.

Wearing stripes, chains, and dreadlocks, giant-sized fugitive Jesse Matthew is returned to Charlottesville to face charges. The law nabbed Jesse from the brink of Mexico, where he was hiding in a pup tent by the waters of Galveston, Texas. That little camping spot is a hot 1,300 miles from his apartment in Charlottesville.

Chief Longo's announcement that Jesse is in custody is not upbeat. He reminds us, with some grimness showing around the corners of his mouth, that we still have a long road, which includes finding Hannah.

In custody, Jesse Matthew gives not an iota of cooperation. He is a stone, unresponsive.

One morning, Dan receives Facebook messages from friends who have superimposed Jesse's photograph on the FBI-enhanced image of Sketch. Oh my God. Everything lines up. It is him.

This is the face of the monster who killed Morgan. We are sure of it. I don't need to wait for the DNA. It's him.

Our understanding of the back-to-school-rapist's criminality shifts. He is the back-to-school murderer, the bone-breaking berserker who kills with his bare hands.

Hannah's remains are found on October 18, 2014, on the 35th day of her being missing. Law enforcement discovers that her body had been tossed in a dry creek bed, on a rural property in wooded Albemarle County, a few miles out of Charlottesville, just down the road from where Jesse grew up, and only five miles from the pasture where Morgan was tossed.

Shortly thereafter, we receive a late night phone call.

It's Virginia State Police.

Special Agent Dino Cappuzzo is calling with a confirmation. "We wanted to tell you as soon as we were certain. Forgive the lateness of our call. We now have a positive DNA link, between the Fairfax abduction/rape/attempted murder case, Hannah's case, and Morgan's. Dr. and Mrs. Harrington, that DNA belongs to Jesse Matthew."

It has taken five molasses years to get to this summit, to have a suspect arrested, and to begin the lengthy legal process of finding justice. I know that the judicial phase is slow and frustrating at times. Regardless, we are so grateful to have the opportunity to fulfill this last parental obligation we have to Morgan, our promise to find her killer.

There have been some bumps on the road to this arrest and justice. The mistake not made, was giving up. No one gave up, not us, not law enforcement, not the media, nor our community and neighbors. We worked together relentlessly to identify the predator in our midst, seeking justice for Morgan, and to prevent her killer's next crime. Despite all our efforts, we were not able to save the next girl.

With Jesse Matthew in custody, our job changes from truth-seeking to observation. It will be up to The Commonwealth of Virginia to determine guilt and punishment and stop his killing spree. I vowed from the beginning of the hearings phase to attend and witness every single court appearance in the convoluted trials of Jesse Matthew, so I write this poem:

Fashion Die-lemma

What to wear?
What do I care
So foolish, in a mess
Can't figure out how to dress

I'm going to meet a killer
Don't want to overdo
Like I dressed up for the rendez-vous
With the guy who murdered you
Want nothing to obscure our pain
So I'll stick with neat and plain
Knowing he'll be sporting stripes and chain

I want to show strength and courage too
How does that translate into a shoe?
Flats will have to do
I want to look composed and calm
Though my mind thrums ALARM
And my very cells clamor for just dis
JUSTICE
I'll emit an unwavering incandescent message of loss and grief
Versus murderer—worst kind of thief

It doesn't matter what I wear
When I'm sitting there
I know this:
I'll be clothed in righteousness
And he'll be unmasked and naked for the world to see
Festering in infamy
And the meter's running, pal
Time to pay up
Fess up
Judgment's coming, and you will atone
For every scream, every moan,
Every snap of broken bone.

Amen
241

———

His hands, his giant ham-hock hands. I am so disturbed by his size, and by the catastrophic size of his assault on my Morgan.

Hand

I see
Jesse
You raised your right hand and swore to tell the truth

I saw your huge right hand, wide across as a dinner plate
Full of hate
I saw your hand and knew it was the hand that killed our daughter, our precious
Morgan
I saw your hand that choked away life, violated flesh

I saw your lowered eyes
They tried to cloak the devastation they had seen, lives lost, skin torn, tears shed,
screams, blood

I saw your eyes
I saw you raise your massive hand to promise truth telling
God knows if you will do/can do so

I only know that I see you clearly

I see you raise your hand
I hear snap of bone
Morgan
I want just dis - justice
The families have all replayed
The snuff films that you made
Starring the back-to-school killer
We don't flinch
We witness
Want dis
Justice

As we enter this phase of trials, seeking justice, I ask Morgan's teacher, Jane Vance, to use her voice to chronicle some of those appearances. I believe Jane's six trial essays show how our long family journey to justice fits into the broader journey of Virginia history. I recognize that truth sometimes prefers riding in the pouch of a story or a description, or waits to be discovered in some unexpected corner of language. I'm hoping that someday, I will catch enough sight of the truth to understand the most elusive and elemental question about Morgan's murderer: why.

I. Crocodile

The first time Gil Harrington saw Jesse Matthew in the flesh was a Monday or a Wednesday, back in the Spring of 2015. I know, because when we drove back from Charlottesville, after sitting 15 feet from him in the courtroom that day, when he stared and stared at Gil, and at Hannah Graham's parents, and at me, I took Gil back to her home in Roanoke, then drove on through a storm up the mountain to Blacksburg, parked along Virginia Tech's Drill Field, and went directly into Randolph Hall to teach my 4-5:15 MW class.

I walked to my car after a wonderful 75 minutes with my students, offering them the same deep ethics and global citizenship I had taught Morgan six Springs before, and by the time I drove ten minutes from campus, reaching my gravel driveway, turning off the ignition, now stopped in the verdant territory of my pink-trumpeted daffodils and heady blue hyacinths, I was really afraid.

Afraid, not because I felt spooked that Jesse Matthew was somehow crouching behind the flowers in my gardens.

He could never camouflage in beauty.

Afraid, because I felt drugged.

I am in my late fifties, very healthy, strong, and happy. This physical fear, as I sat in my parked car, wondering whether I was going to be able to walk the 30 steps to get into my house, was something I had read about but never experienced.

I felt as if I had been hit by a poisoned dart.

I thought I would have to sleep on the ground, somewhere between my car and my door. No exaggeration. I got inside, and still in my clothes, and in my shoes, I slept. Until morning. When I woke, and showered, and drank my hot tea, I remember looking at my hands and being surprised that they were not covered in boils or bruises, that my skin was unchanged, undiseased.

I wasn't sore. My ribs weren't hurt. My back was strong. I could move my jaws and swallow. I drove to work. Where was the poison? I remember feeling a little embarrassed to mention to Gil, when we spoke later that day, that I had been, as I did put it to her, wiped out, the night before.

Dan and Gil Harrington are the most empathetic people I have ever known. So even if I had needed to talk about myself, and even if I were histrionic, Gil would have put my trouble into context, and helped coax me down from that unstable highest branch of the tree.

I didn't want to sound like my experience the day before was such a big deal, given the circumstance that Gil Harrington and John and Sue Graham had just, for the first time, sat in close proximity to the suspected brutal murderer of both their daughters, Morgan and Hannah. But I told Gil. And I did not expect her response. She explained that as soon as I left, that early afternoon, she had stretched out on her living room carpet, maybe just to rest her back after the car ride.

That's where Dan found her, hours later, when he came home from work. Splayed, sprawled flat out on the floor. Still deeply asleep. As if she had been hit by a poisoned dart.

I told Gil: it's as if Jesse Matthew's presence, that first time, was itself a date rape drug, one which he emits, and which we inhaled, just by being in the room with him. Or, it's as if we had had to induce our own comas, to repair our shock. We had been near something so unfamiliar, so unnatural, so appalling, not because he grimaces or smirks or leers--he doesn't--but because he is so calm and still, so like a Mexican Day of the Dead Judas figure, bigger than life-sized, lumpy, a giant heavy papier-mâché man, but breathing. As Gil says, I have no receptors for what he is.

Escorted by armed guards, Jesse toddled in. He was in ankle chains, handcuffs, and a prison constraint we had never heard of: a belly chain. This chain shackled his wrists to his abdomen.

My God. A 33-year-old man, jangling in chains. Although there are a pitcher and cups on the table, Jesse can't pour himself a glass of water. He can't raise his hand to swear the truth, the whole truth, and nothing but the truth. The implication is clear. He can't kill anyone in court.

Gil and I are dressed in black, for the occasion, both of us wearing cantaloupe orange scarves, for Hannah Graham, her favorite color. Jesse is dressed in a stiff prison jump suit. Gil notes: ironically, it is orange, too. Jesse's long dreads are loose. They swing when he walks, but once he is seated, nothing about him moves.

The size of Jesse Matthew brings terrible images to life.

The Judge does not recuse herself. Yes, she has a daughter who attends UVA, but the sage judge does not find reason to think she can't be a fair judge for this trial.

Hannah Graham's trial dates are set: July 5 to July 29, but not this year. Hannah's trial begins in July, 2016. A year away. The months swing like prison chains. I see the long stretch of legal delay punch Gil in the gut. Jesse cuts his eyes at us. Observing him today, the back of my mind still paged through every book and article I've ever absorbed, from 1960s Childcraft encyclopedia folk tales, where I learned about wickedness, to research on ice-blooded psychopaths. In Jesse Matthew's presence, I race with myself to find something, anything that he resembles, but each time, I am baffled. Each time, I sense that I've never been in a presence like his. His expressionlessness unsettles. What else is alive but makes no shift whatsoever in its expression?

What else is electric with hidden pounce?

Octopi, until they surge to grab food. Lions and leopards and tigers and cheetahs, before they accelerate. And sexual predators.

This one, we've seen caught on video camera. Traipsing with his bourbon gut, padding in the bad fashion of those blousy shorts that hang from his middle like pillow cases, he moves as dull as sleeping quicksand. Until he sees Hannah. Then, as we know, his motion explodes. He hairpin turns, lengthens his stride, and glides like hell. I see something else, too, from that night. It's nothing I could report to Charlottesville Police Chief Longo. But look, look with me at the camera's still capture. This is Jesse Matthew, seconds before he shifts gear, and already, his shadow is making freakish suggestions.

If you really look at this still image from the night Hannah Graham went missing, as a child or an artist will look, and if you'll be willing to see the shapes of things, allowing the trompe l'oeil, you'll see the trick of the evening: Jesse Matthew looks as if he is riding, balanced, on the tip of a crocodile's snout, the way every baby crocodile in fact does like to ferry on his mother. Do you see it? Look again. Perhaps by accident, his shadow is shaped like a crocodile. Jesse's phantom reptile is channeling him to the perfect spot, just across the brick river, where he can leap off, and snap for himself.

These days, we have to count how many times we've sat near Jesse in court. And we've noticed, since his Fairfax defeat: all his latent volition is shriveling. Like a dying dragon whose lungs are dead campfires, his breath across the room, Jesse's very presence now, like a musty antiquated bellows, now blows nothing concentrated. We can breathe, stay awake, sometimes even eat a few bites of a meal, after proximity to him. His presence, at least in the confines of the courtroom, no longer completely debilitates.

But, still, I sense residual poison and power in the company of Jesse Matthew. Yet I know the Angels have banished his vehicle, not just that fateful cab he used to drive, but his abysmal shadow-vehicle, this alligator-shape you see protruding up from the bottom of the photograph, the one who has given Jesse his primitive lift. And unlike the Gingerbread Boy, who trusted riding the nose of that conniving fox, and who was devoured, Jesse, who rode a kindred beast, remains. And the cold-blooded rhyme of Jesse Matthew runs grim:

Run, run, as fast as you can,
You can't stop me,
I'm the Crocodile Man!

I ride the nose of a shadowy beast;
We troll on the mall
'til I smell a feast.

I'm propelled to her side
On my crocodile ride,
Unconcerned about law in the least.

Run, run, but my reach is vaster.
Try, try, but my fists are faster.
My crocodile guide
And my long practiced stride
Mean tonight is a tasty disaster.

Run, swim, flail, fight.
The Crocodile Man has weight and bite.
You are nothing but prey.
I will throw you away, and--

Since crocodile--
Is in my blood

And I know ditches, brush, and mud,
And field and cab, and mall and car,
And John Paul Jones and Tempo Bar,
And I have shadows who will ride me
Propel, deliver, taxi-glide me,
Put me where the victims are,
Those shiny twinkle twinkle stars,

Who make me snap
And snap again,
And glut myself on girly sin,

I will always ride with hunger.
I will always pull them under.

In secluded gloaming time,
I will always make them mine.

Stop me if you ever can, but
I am Crocodile--more than man.

II. Seven Dispatches to Mr. Jefferson

I.

Dear Thomas,

I have artist-eyes, sensitive to details and changes. Almost imperceptibly, just for a second, the thinning, flyaway strands behind your left ear moved today, ever so slightly. That's how I found you. It's the cleverest place for a ghost to have hidden, in the portrait of his own countenance.

Whereas the Honorable Judge Cheryl Higgins' work required her eyes to follow Prosecutors Denise Lunsford, Carrene Walker, Matt Quatrara, special agents Michal Arcoraci, Dino Cappuzzo, and Defense attorney Doug Ramseur, and occasionally to consult her open laptop or case book, I noticed your unblinking gaze remained on Jesse Matthew and his mother. Because of how naughty it is for you to be attending Jesse Matthew's hearings, secretly--a presidential ghost, spying, really; haunting your own old Albemarle County Courthouse--I feel liberated from formalities. So I hope it's alright that I won't be addressing you as President Jefferson.

Nothing irreverent intended. It's just that, on a first-name basis, maybe we can talk. I'd like the chance to see through your eyes. I want to think with you about the extraordinary moment we witnessed.

Jane Lillian Vance

II.

Dear Thomas,

Let me assure you that I have thought about you before today. Since we were in the Courtroom to consider a man's troubles, let me tell you what I know about yours. Your former Vice President, Mr. Burr, my God. Scandalous, that he needed to be tried for treason. Worse, that he was a murderer. Did he really want to take over the western states, and lead an unauthorized invasion of Mexico? And did you ever think that he wanted to duel with you more than with Alexander Hamilton? If you ask me, you were lucky.

Indelicate, that you enacted the Indian Tribal Removal Act, to clear the Louisiana Purchase of indigenous people. We call that expedience genocide.

Redeeming, when you originated the Act to Prohibit the Importation of Slaves. Unlovely, though, when by day you so eloquently decried slavery, and by night, in that little room on the steep hill growing the bitter rhubarb and dusky cabbages, you bedded Sally Hemings, whom you owned. And disgraceful that, for almost 200 years, the remains of your Jefferson-Hemings' descendants were denied burial near your seed-corpse.

Listing your limitations, though, I know we are all besieged by our own imperfections. But they are nothing, a mere cloud of gnats, against the clear sky of one shining moment of pure compassion.

I'm glad you saw it happen. I can't stop thinking about it.

Jane

III.

Dear Thomas,

The 14th Dalai Lama, the spiritual leader of Tibet, had to flee an assassination attempt in 1959. He walked for 19 days, with fever and dysentery, over frozen rivers with red wolves howling nearby, to reach the safety of the Indian border.

Thirty years later, he was awarded a Nobel Peace Prize. A quarter-century after that recognition, he is possibly the most admired person in the world. He keeps trying to find common ground with his nation's occupiers and his personal antagonists and detractors. He has never been able to go home.

Long trial + spiritual wisdom + resilience = what would you call it?

The Dalai Lama has said: "Non-violence takes a long time."

Maybe the best characterization of what we saw happen in court today is non-violence. Or is it courage? How can we name it? As a Christian Deist, what would you call it? Grace?

Jane

IV.

Dear Thomas,

Listen, I'm assuming you know you're dead? I don't know how well you've followed history--I mean, what would have been the future--after your patriotic death on July 4th, 1826. So I don't know how well you understand who the Dalai Lama is. Or Mahatma Gandhi--the little man, the non-politician, who, employing brilliant, coordinated, nonviolent civil disobedience, helped long-suffering, colonized India secure her Independence from the British, on the stroke of midnight, August 16th, 1947. I know: that was 121 years too late for you to celebrate.

Both of these men came to my mind, given what we saw in court today.

Religious figures, mystics, and warriors-turned-healers, did too: all the merciful emissaries, St. Francis of Assisi, Pope Francis, Mother Teresa, Rumi, Emperor Ashoka, Siddhartha, Aung San Suu Kyi, Alice Walker, Maya Angelou, Jesus Christ. They all tried, or try their best, to be resilient, determined, holy. For me, holiness is practical.

Th at's because the best secular behavior and the best sacred tenets always find each other and join forces. One is always becoming the other, and each is each. And the absence of one is also the absence of the other. Therefore, for example, if you're a jerk, you pontificate instead of teach. You can't be both arrogant and fair. You can't be temperamentally angry and loving. If you are kind, you are helpful. If you are forgiving, you heal. And you can't be a wonderful serial rapist and murderer.

But what about being a mother, and crossing the courtroom to lean forward and speak to the other mother, whose son murdered your daughter? Did you, in your time, have a category for that magnitude of remarkable being? Her name is Gil Harrington.

Jane

V.

Dear Thomas,

After Gil's daughter Morgan was murdered, she and her gentle, magnanimous husband, Dan--you saw him, Morgan's father--went to the beach where Morgan had loved to swim.

Gil told me that she realized the beach on which she was standing--which she had only ever thought of as the beach--was made of trillions of grains of broken things. She had only seen sand before. But now, after Morgan's murder, Gil saw that she stood on an endless stretch of impermanence. The grains were infinitesimal remains, of massive rocks, and lobster claws; of nautilus shells, and red coral; of archaeopteryx teeth, and urchin spines. And perhaps, in the breeze, there are also infinitesimal remains, tiny fragments of distant sounds from a forgotten or undiscovered past.

Sound-sand.

Perhaps, when your Lewis and Clark reached the Pacific, having collected that fine hunk of mastodon jaw, which is still displayed at your Monticello, and so many other great fossils and artifacts for you, Kwakiutl and Lakota things, and drawings of rivers and mountains, perhaps, like Gil Harrington on the beach, they had a sense of how much had come before them which was now reduced to particles of sand.

Perhaps Lewis and Clark heard fleeting remnant notes of Tibetan cymbals and horns drifting like ghostly sound-particles from a vital culture and an unimaginably beautiful landscape, beyond even the ocean they had struggled for so long to reach.

Gil told me she was undaunted.

For her, it wasn't a depressing realization that the sand was made of broken things. Instead, she realized that you can leave things broken, or you can change and use them. You can meld and clarify them. You can take sand, and make glass. Her mind, I think, is not unlike the part of yours I admire, Thomas: the planter, the inventor, the propagator.

Jane

VI.

Dear Thomas,

All these thoughts, I hope, contextualize the main point. Gil Harrington rose from her place on the wooden bench, facing your portrait hanging there just over Judge Higgins' head, and, against the current of all expectation, and not because of anyone's particular expectation one way or another, alone and without precedent or external guidance, she walked to stand before Jesse Matthew's mother. I walked with her. So I saw as you also saw. Jesse Matthew's mother was still seated. She looked up at Gil. There was suffering in her face. She has a sweet face. But there was long suffering there.

Gil and I have seen that look in some of the patients we've helped in Zambia. An expression so used to difficulties that a slap would be more expected than a kindness. Her son Jesse is charged with the murder of Gil's daughter--not his only murder charge or other horrible crime. Gil said, face to face, and leaning in to Jesse's mother, "I realize that this is difficult for your family as well. My condolences." And then Gil extended her hand.

I swear time stopped.

Even God gasped.

It took a noticeable pause, and in that pause, Jesse's mother glanced to the right and to the left of her, disbelieving that whoever was with her was also witnessing this moment. And then she raised her hand. Not as her son had done to Morgan. Jesse's mother, in her nice brown dress, raised her gentle hand and took Gil's sweet hand. These two women were connected for the first time.

They held one another for a few seconds.

And in those seconds, I saw Jesse's mother's face contort away from an old stoic stare into a wincing, and then finally a relieved and overcome smile. She said, barely audibly, Thank you. Gil returned the smile, and we walked out of the Courtroom.

Reuters, Associated Press, CBS, everyone got wind of what had just happened. Gil was walking over to speak to a hundred microphones.

But in an interstice before she did, Gil and I watched Jesse Matthew's mother walk away, receding down a side street, more slowly and more at ease than we had ever seen her leave before. And then, when I looked back at Gil, my heart sank. I was at first afraid.

I don't know what you ghosts can see, Thomas. Maybe you see us carry an aura or crown of emotions we don't even know we're capable of shining, abilities and feelings we don't even recognize we own. I saw something in Gil's face, mostly in her eyes. I'm not sure how often people achieve this expression. Gil was alchemizing.

I saw the poison she had just absorbed. She had absorbed it from Jesse's mom. And as an immunization gives you a little bit of the disease to cause a reaction to it, Gil had caught Jesse's mother's agony. I saw those moments.

I know my friend Gil, and I saw her changed with the agony of Jesse's mother. She was, for a few seconds, broken as two mothers. And then I saw her transform that agony. She took it in, reacted to it, and was well again. But something had changed. Not just in Gil. In Jesse's mother, too. I think you call this alchemy a healing.

Jane

VII.

Dear Thomas,

Go back up the mountain, now. I'm sure you sleep at Monticello, if ghosts sleep. I'm guessing, in Sally's quarters. I suspect you see now better than you could then that you actually deeply loved her. I'm glad I spotted you today. You would think that discovering the ghost of Thomas Jefferson hiding in a Jesse Matthew motions hearing would be my headline. But really, it's unsurprising that you were there, and really, you know what we saw.

I know in 1803 you called the Albemarle Courthouse the "Common Temple" for Charlottesville and the County. I know you hung out on the court square with James Madison and James Monroe, talking about the rights of the individual, both a Jesse Matthew and a Morgan Harrington.

The Courtroom is now listed on the National Registry of Historic Places. But today it became more historic. For a reason I know you understand. The Latin word *taberna* gives birth to two other words, both *tavern* and *tabernacle*. *Taberna* means shed, a place of tools; stall, a shelter for beasts; workshop, where tools are forged; and pub, where joy and celebration join work. In your day, and ages before you, Thomas Jefferson, a tabernacle and a tavern were both places of sanctuary and adoration, not ironically, but brilliantly.

Intoxicating and detoxifying.

Today, the Albemarle Courthouse was all taberna, wasn't it.

Gil changed bad blood to holy wine, and sacrifice to sacrament. Maybe you ghosts know when miracles are about to happen, and you come for the show. Wasn't it a fine transubstantiation in the Common Temple.

Best I've ever seen.

Amen.

Love,

Jane

III. Celestial

National, even global--the increasing responses to Jesse Matthew's murder charges are relatively quantifiable. The national and global responses are, to summarize: big, and getting bigger. Type in Morgan Harrington, and the Google engine today identifies twelve million, three hundred thousand results. Morgan's Facebook is two million. Her Mom yields 628,000 hits.

And as for the Foundation Gil Harrington founded to eradicate predatory danger, search Help Save the Next Girl and you'll see 524,000,000: that's five hundred and twenty four MILLION hits. That's more than half a BILLION. But there is another response to The Day of Charges--which occurred on the very day, September 15th, when Jesse Matthew was served charges for murdering Morgan. This is a response whose category is, for want of an exact identification, something else. It isn't local, or national, or even global. This response is the 45th of its kind. At least, Gil started taking pictures 45 instances ago, after she realized how many were happening.

We call the response Birdstrike.

Although the Harringtons have lived in their home for 25 years, they never once had a bird smash into one of their windows. Never before--until Morgan's murder. Since then, the Harringtons' home--I've heard it happen myself 15 times--continues to be surprised by incoming Birdstrikes. A bird comes flying at one of the Harringtons' windows, smashes full force into the glass, but never, not once, breaks its neck and dies, or even lands below, temporarily stunned or disoriented. The Birdstrikes happen on both sides of the house, and not only on windows that are by line of sight clearly connected to other windows. Again, these strikes have happened only since Morgan's murder. And to no other homes in their neighborhood. We've asked. So the 45th Birdstrike, since Gil decided to start keeping records of them, happened--can you imagine? It happened on the very morning of Jesse Matthew's new charges, just a few hours before Gil received the call from Albemarle County Commonwealth's Prosecutor, alerting Gil that papers were about to be served.

SMACK!

Gil heard the THUD of another Birdstrike. Kirby started barking. The Birdstrikes are loud. This one was on her dining room window. She called me, amazed: "Jane! This one is the most beautiful, the most fully expressed Birdstrike yet." They are visible, because they leave a kind of powdery impression on the glass. And whereas you might expect a smudge, or sections of the impact to be smudged, these Birdstrikes are always in clear, exquisite focus.

This new Birdstrike showed both arms completely outstretched, and, strange to say, but you can see for yourself: the bird seemed to be--I hesitate to phrase my observation--the bird seemed to be smiling.

Gil takes photographs of the Birdstrikes at night, by cell phone flash or flashlight. She enhances nothing about them. They are the actual marks left by birds who apparently have smacked straight into glass and inexplicably were completely unharmed and casually flew away. None of which ever happened before Morgan's murder.

Today, Gil sent me the image of the newest Birdstrike. The one from the very morning the Commonwealth's Office in Charlottesville was finalizing the hand-delivery of charges for Jesse Matthew in Morgan Harrington's murder case. Whatever Heaven is, if the Birdstrikes are its calling cards, delivered by unharmed messengers, its beings are peaceful, wouldn't you agree?

Like sheep in a sheepfold, protected now from devastation, and especially from marauders, from the evil of plunderers, predators, rapists and murderers. Which reminds me of a beautiful saying: When you lie down among the sheepfolds, you are like the wings of a dove covered in silver, and its pinions with glistening gold. Isn't it a pretty idea that peaceful beings, protected by safe surrounds, are like angels, with dazzling wings.

That saying is Psalms 68:13. Our hearts glisten, too, as we marvel at the winged mystery of Morgan's own response.

IV. The Visitation

I don't know the visiting hours and I don't know which prison will be Jesse Matthew's.

Unless he pleads guilty, he may be a relatively brief visitor himself, assigned along the infamous gray row where dead men beyond rehabilitation walk out of their cells to their scheduled execution. I don't know how many appeals will carry Jesse Matthew aloft on his remaining apocalyptic months of concrete and chains--his lawn and flowers.

During his incarceration, who from among the living will visit this man that I believe will be proven an infamous sexual predator and serial killer, becoming a terrible memory in criminal justice lectures, indelibly featured in cramped dozens of jail-faced Google images?

Family, I guess, will at first make the dreary pilgrimage, but how can the conversation run? How have you been, Jesse? We're all fine. No, nothing much has changed. Well, except that there seem to be fewer skeletonized girls found in the Albemarle woods.

Like kissing an electric fence, those live visits will burn: they will always burn, and the puckered keloids will never heal. So Jesse Matthew's human visits will thin, thin to the vanishing point. Which will suit his other visitors.

In every one of the thirty-three countries where I've traveled, without exception, I have met rational, high-functioning, sane people, who, with no fixations on horror films or grim folklore, and no embarrassment or ambivalence, accept the existence of ghosts. The purpose, powers, and the forms of ghosts do vary, culturally, but ghosts, I have gathered, are ubiquitous.

There are those we might call Good Ghosts, who assist the living. We refer to them as Angels. They leave enigmatic directions we might call coincidences, and if you can see to follow their messages, you find medicine, secret passageways, and insights.

The Good Ghosts usually knew us when they were alive; we loved them, and now they protect and guide us. They lose their inhibitions most when we are dreaming; they come and play with us then, hide and seek and riddle games, as if we are all children together. Violence in your heart sends Good Ghosts away, and once banished, they cannot remember you. There are other Ghosts as well.

Universally, Angry Ghosts don't like to be observed by a crowd, so they haunt solitary but not entirely empty places, where there is usually just one person to witness or hear their presence, like an inmate in a prison cell. Angry Ghosts are inclined to show themselves where they are positive no one else can detect them, enter and reside, like a hidden roommate, in the deep interior of secretive, guilty minds, where not even an exorcism can dislodge them. In his nocturnal prison room, like cockroaches, Angry Ghosts may soon scuttle around Jesse's isolated mind.

No one should pleasure in the punishments wrought by an infestation of Angry Ghosts. They are inhumane, and relentless. Like fleas or ticks, the Angry Ghosts bite, pinch, fill themselves, and lay eggs. They are horrors, fueled by the venom of retaliation. They destroy peace.

There is another rare and unusual specter.

A Phoenix, a reincarnated ghost, is alive again as a human, so she is not exactly a ghost. But she was, like a drowned woman who spews the water from her lungs and coughs back to respiration, for all intents and purposes, dead, and then not dead. You could call a Phoenix just a survivor, but the ghosts always claim her as one of theirs. She tagged their realm, and she has powers that other people do not. To be in the presence of the Phoenix, RG, who sputtered back to life from Jesse Matthew's strangling, Gil Harrington and I returned to the Fairfax Circuit Courtroom on this afternoon, June 18, 2015.

RG is the young woman who was attacked in 2005 while carrying her groceries home. For ten years she had been understandably reluctant to detail the full extent of her attempted murder, until she sat before Judge Schell on the first day of the Fairfax trial. On the witness stand, she mastered liberation. Unlocking her own prison, she admitted outright that in fact Jesse Matthew had fully raped her. And any doubt about her powers as a Phoenix dissolved when, just two days later, after the prosecutors proved their case-- "overwhelmingly," to quote Judge Schell--and Jesse Matthew pled guilty, she requested to reconvene the court specifically to have her day, to speak before the prosecuting and defense teams, before the Judge AND Jesse Matthew, in an open courtroom, before dozens of live-streaming reporters, and explain exactly what suffering and impact, for a decade, Jesse Matthew's wildly brutal, diseased attack has caused. That day was today.

You must realize: just to enter the Fairfax County Circuit Court, exactly as though you were proceeding through security at an airport, one has to proceed through a zigzag line, remove one's shoes, and, if you wear a dazzle of rings and bracelets as Gil and I prefer, get wanded. Blue digital schedule boards hang high from the walls and announce five dozen cases being heard throughout the building, as if they were an abundance of flights. Such a clockwork space would not be where I expected to behold a living ghost today, but in she walked. I had somehow imagined a quavering statement, delivered despite sniffles. Clearly, I had never fathomed a Phoenix.

RG has the casual command of a woman gifted in languages and cross-cultural pleasures. She is physically slight, but metaphysically executive. RG was dressed powerfully nonchalantly, in casual western chic, an elegant, slender presence. Having crossed oceans to return to Fairfax, she inhaled after a decade's nightmares, swore her identity on the stand, and flared her tremendous Phoenix wings.

Yes, she indicated, she could barely pick up a cup, move from a chair, walk across a room, or chew food, after he brutalized her. She was so badly beaten, broken with pain. Yes, she wrestled with self-esteem. And she tried, as she said, to put what Jesse Matthew had done to her "in cold storage"; to repress how she had thought, in the moments of struggle, so this is how I will die. I am dying. My life is ending now.

And she realized: as she tried to hide from these memories, she eroded. She without action in response to his crimes was eroding. So the Phoenix rose to vibrant being. She called her attacker a faceless parasite. She recognized the scourge of such violent sexual predators, and spoke on behalf of all victims, everywhere in the world, to protect and defend them. She recognized the heroism of the American judicial system which persisted on her behalf for a decade.

She confirmed that she relives the horrible attack every day; suffers the shock of a man, then 23, smashing, beating, strangling, and raping her. She thought no one would hear her cries, and that Jesse Matthew would extinguish her.

Judge Schell was at full profile to the courtroom. He was entirely focused on her testimony. He watched the Phoenix intently. She finished her work, and walked out. And then, wearing a convict's dull green prison jumpsuit, Jesse Matthew, who had watched RG's testimony as unresponsively as if he were a stale loaf of bread, as nondescript as a cinder block, as odd as a styrofoam mannequin with toothpaste for blood; cold, unnatural, a bad approximation of a man, Jesse Matthew was led out, to be whisked to Charlottesville, where he has other trials descending like tornadoes. After the formal courtroom appearance of RG, post-docket, the Phoenix had another request.

So down the hall and through two doors, Gil and I were lead, flanked by armed deputies, the prosecutors, and the victim's advocacy assistants. In a small room, RG entered. How can I tell you the magic of being in such proximity to the girl who came back to life.

What a historic meeting, all of us trembling a little, finally to have flown to this rare branch of mutual minutes to say we had been aware of one another for years, and to hug, and to hold each other's hands. Gil was so glad to embrace RG. I was so glad to take her hands in my hands, and to kiss her on the cheek. She was warm as fire, this reincarnate. She was smart, and happy, and she also had a tremble, a little quaver to one side of her smile, like a little earthquake beginning, or a new molting.

We were covered in phoenix feathers and redemption.

There is one final chapter to the First Trial of Jesse Matthew. Tomorrow, a different specter has work to do, who is not a Phoenix. In the Epilogue, a different class of Ghost speaks to Jesse Matthew.

Her name is Morgan.

V. The Beatitudes

Revered among Angels are the most powerful specters of all the heavens: they are called the Beauties, and with immeasurable tenderness and constancy, they watch over their anguished loved ones.

Noble despite their own tragic deaths, the Beauties are the victims of murderers, terrible illnesses, or shocking and sudden accidents.

Their lost potential is regained and amplified a billion fold. They occupy the entire sky, see the sweetness of human desires, encourage lovers, breathe the perfume of gardens, love clouds, music, dance, and human eloquence.

They love to see endeavors: carpenters drive home nails, writers edit, window washers make the glass squeak. They love to see advocates: public school teachers empowering young students to watch out for one another's safety, t-shirts worn to spread a good idea, scarves and ribbons and bracelets chosen because their colors represent a beloved who is gone.

They watch their families continue to pick up forks and spoons and put their heads on pillows to wake to another day without them.

Earnestness and persistence make them applaud. They know that the highest calling of human beings is service. They know that mechanics and lawyers can be as full of kind assistance as librarians and doctors. They know that some healers requires oil paint or stained glass, and others, circular saws or dental drills. They are in love with the world.

The murdered Beauties lead this rare group.

They appear before their fretful murderers in the dead of night and wake them, considerately. They aren't beyond sympathy for their murderers, and know that their arrival will be almost heart-stopping.

Picture Morgan Harrington, for example, sitting beside Jesse on his cell palette, her pals Hannah, Alexis, Annalee, Sage, and Nicole standing around her.

"Jesse," she'll squeeze his arm gently, "Wake up, Jesse."

He remembers her.

"Yes," she smiles, "You remember me. No," she answers his next thought, before he speaks it, smiling at the primitive fear, "I'm not here to strangle you."

And before he can formulate the words, she answers: "I don't want anything. I take care of the people you hurt when you murdered me. I just need you to see something. I need you to see what you killed."

"I see you! I see you!," Jesse pleads, like a modern Scrooge.

"No, Jesse," Morgan instructs, smiling to herself that she was going to be a teacher and here she is, teaching the slowest kid in the cell, "There's more."

Looking into The Beauty's eyes, Jesse is swept away from his cell.

He sees himself in his cab that night, seeing Morgan, but he is distracted by a group of laughing kids, who cluster and block his view of Morgan. Morgan goes home.

For what seems the rest of his life, Morgan shows Jesse what he killed.

She shows him her wedding, her children, their first words. He sees her go to Zambia and teach the poorest children on the continent. He sees Morgan's blonde-headed babies dancing with Zambian children with brave names, Charity, Lioness, Gift, and Purity. The children move lightly and fast like butterflies.

Morgan's three daughters all look like their grandmama, Gil. He hears their names: Danielle, Gilberte, and Alexis. Her son looks just like his grandpapa, Dan. What's his name? Jesse wants to ask, involved now in this diaphanous story, but the little boy's name always seems drowned out by laughter.

He is the sunniest, most loving little boy, with grass-stained toes and alluring green eyes. He loves people, and even as a young boy he understands trust and loss. He cries when his neighbor's dog dies of cancer. He draws a picture of the dog walking on a rainbow and meeting God on the other side.

Morgan shows Jesse Matthew her family vacations to climb the Swiss Alps with her cousins. She stays with her friends Emerson and Ariel in D.C.; they travel to the Great Wall of China together. Her friends Iris and David take her to Sri Lanka and Nepal. Their friend Ian is there with his partner. Morgan admires their matching emerald rings, and has one made for her best friend, Erin. Morgan's children cannonball into the pool at Helga's Folly. They all sit and drink fresh lime sodas together under the crazy pomelo trees in the Kathmandu Guest House garden.

Morgan's children are teenagers now, almost ready for college. They have strong preferences. Danielle, the oldest, wants to be an oncology nurse. Gilberte is an artist. Alexis wants to live in New York and do fashion design, and live with her famous uncle, her hero.

Morgan's little boy, growing up, says he had always thought he wanted to be a doctor, but when he is 16, he cannot deny that he has had a calling, to be a priest. He says he must have inherited his grandpapa's faith. He wants to be like Christ, healing the broken-hearted.

Morgan supports them all.

She skips to the ceremony when her grown son graduates from Divinity School and takes his robes and collar. He will now be called Father.

"I've just received word," her new priest confides as he hugs his beautiful mother. Morgan will soon celebrate her 50th birthday. "I got the job, Mama. I'll be working in Fairfax. There is a lot of anger in the suburbs. I think we can reach a lot of kids."

Morgan, with tears streaming down both sides of her gorgeous middle-aged face, pulls her tender-hearted son from this celebratory embrace. She smiles, and with pride and admiration, confirms, "Yes, my handsome son, I always knew you would." She stares at the extraordinary, devotional light in his kind eyes, and hugs her son again. "I love you, Father Jesse."

At this moment, the visiting Beauties are all smiling at Jesse Matthew, who is propped on his cell palette. He notices that their shadows are incandescent, like cool, evenly burning white shapes of female fire. He cannot fathom Morgan's loving eyes, and he is surprised when her ghost, who seems so human, though smiling at him, also has tears running down her insubstantial face.

He is crying himself.

"Don't go!" He begs.

But at that exact moment, the Beauties, with pity in their gentle smiles, their work done, all disappear.

To him, they will never return.

Only his memories of Morgan as a Beauty and the others alongside her, Annalee, with her rainbow streak of hair and the design of a jumping horse glowing over her heart, Alexis in pink lipstick, with fine, lean, 17-year-old muscular arms, Hannah, tall and cheerful, her 18-year-old smile scintillating, Sage, the brave transgender ghost, beautiful to all, 13-year-old Nicole, wearing her pink cowgirl boots and cradling her toy panda, and the legacies of Morgan's family, which he also killed, the faces of these children who were never born, and their bright contributions, remain for him.

In their radiance, and in their radiance vanishing and lost, never to return, never again to wake him softly, they are, for the rest of his life, the worst, and by far the most painful haunting of Jesse Matthew.

VIRGINIA: IN THE CIRCUIT COURT OF THE COUNTY OF ALBEMARLE ON THE CRIMINAL SIDE THEREOF, HELD ON **MARCH 2, 2016.**

PRESENT: HON. **CHERYL V. HIGGINS**

COMMONWEALTH OF VIRGINIA

VS.

JESSE LEROY MATTHEW, JR.

Sex: male
DOB: 12/14/1981   Race: black
STATUS: jail

Case Number	Offense	VCC Code	F/M	Offense Date	Virginia Code Section
15-52	Abduction with Intent to Defile	KID-1004-F2	F	09/13/2014	18.2-48
15-53	First Degree Murder	MUR-0925-F2	F	09/13/2014	18.2-32
15-54	Reckless Driving/Speed	REC-6646-M1	M	09/20/2014	46.2-862
15-55	Reckless Driving/Other	REC-6641-M1	M	09/20/2014	46.2-857
15-247	Capital Murder: During Abduction	MUR-0913-F1	F	09/13/2014	18.2-31(1)
15-516	First Degree Murder	MUR-0925-F2	F	10/17/2009	18.2-32
15-517	Abduction with Intent to Defile	KID-1004-F2	F	10/17/2009	18.2-48

Attorney for the Commonwealth: Robert N. Tracci, Matthew Quatrara & Carrene Walker

Attorney for the Defendant: David Ramseur, Michael Hemenway and Katherine Jensen

The defendant was present with his attorneys.

On motion of the Attorney for the Commonwealth and in accordance with a ***plea agreement*** now filed in this matter, it is Ordered that indictments #15-54, #15-55 and #15-247 be nolle prossed.

The accused was arraigned and after private consultation with and being advised by his said counsel and in accordance with a *plea agreement* now filed in this case, pleaded guilty to the Indictments, which pleas were tendered by the accused in person, and the Court, having made inquiry and being of the opinion that the accused fully understood the nature and effect of his pleas and of the penalties that may be imposed upon his conviction and of the waiver of trial by jury and of appeal, and finding that his pleas were voluntarily and intelligently made, proceeded to hear and determine the case and having heard the evidence and argument of counsel, the Court finds the defendant GUILTY as charged in the Indictments.

The Attorney for the Commonwealth and the defendant were given the opportunity to present evidence pertaining to sentencing.

Pursuant to the provisions of Virginia Code Section 19.2-298.01, the Court has considered the applicable discretionary sentencing guidelines and the guidelines worksheets.

Before pronouncing the sentence, the Court inquired if the defendant desired to make a statement and if the defendant desired to advance any reasons why judgment should not be pronounced.

The Court SENTENCED the defendant to incarceration with the Virginia Department of Corrections for the term of *Life as to indictment #15-52, Life as to indictment #15-53, Life as to indictment #15-516, and Life as to indictment #15-517.*

SENTENCING SUMMARY:

TOTAL SENTENCE IMPOSED: *Four Life Sentence*

Pursuant to the Plea agreement, the defendant agreed to waive his right and ability to request or petition for any form of conditional release, early release, or parole, such as geriatric conditional release currently codified in Virginia Code Section 53.1-40.01.

COURT COSTS. The defendant shall pay Court costs.

This sentence shall run *consecutively* to any other sentences imposed.

The Court certifies that at all times during the trial of this case the defendant was personally present and counsel for the defendant was personally present.

ENTER: _____
                        JUDGE

DATE: _3-18-16_____

a true copy TESTE:
JON K. ZUG, CLERK
by: _____
          Deputy Clerk

VI. No More Trials: Justice at Last

Charlottesville, Virginia

March 3, 2016

Today, after six and a half diligent years, Justice completes her marathon pursuit.

Predators are--thank God--very, very rare. Brutal serial killers are really rare, almost non-existent. But not quite.

The explanation of sweet Morgan's and Hannah's murders is, finally, sickeningly and heartbreakingly casual: Jesse was simply being true to his nature.

Jesse Matthew was a deceptively calm pursuit artist, who had had great success in satisfying his terrible needs.

Now, like Goliath, Jesse has fallen.

His danger to other young women is completely finished.

Fallen before in Fairfax, he fell today, for the last time, receiving four new life sentences, two for brutally abducting and murdering Hannah, and two for brutally abducting and murdering Morgan, seven now in total.

The Albemarle Courthouse was packed and bristling on this day of long sought culmination. Judge Higgins asked: "Are you pleading guilty because you are in fact guilty of the crimes?"

With his enormous back to us, chained and broadened by wide black and white prison stripes, Jesse Matthew confessed, "Yes, ma'am."

He has avoided the death penalty, but, starting tonight, when the sun seems to sink, it is really Jesse who will begin sinking, and who will have no choice but to recede into his shallow, separate, dark box of insignificance.

As today's plea agreement took pains to establish, he will never, not for any reason, emerge from prison.

Heartfelt thanks to the skillful finesse and compassion of Commonwealth's Attorney Robert Tracci and his team. They recognized and sought the finality and accountability that a plea agreement offered the victims' families. None of us need to be wary of this particular lethal predator ever again.

That fact is a blessing, but nothing about Jesse's crimes and, equally, nothing about his sentencing is joyful. No one who attended could characterize the day of Jesse Matthew's sentencing as celebratory.

It was long overdue relief. It was correct. It was solemn. It was final. But it was not happy making. The four life sentences he received could not resurrect the two lives he took. Those crimes cannot be undone, so the protection that Jesse's forever incarceration brings to the community must suffice. No winners here, only the promise of safety for the next girl.

Please recall that miracles are always, have always been available, but you have to see them, and choose them. You have to participate to conjure and receive a miracle. After you have witnessed them, you realize that miracles are, to be exact, corrections of bad habits. Miracles save us, and today was a day of miracles. From the beginning, Gil Harrington has consistently worked to safe-keep the next girl, not to unleash retribution and bloody vengeance. Gil has always chosen against obstacles.

Today, Gil chose the direct path to miracles, and with my own eyes, I saw the blessing arrive.

Before the murderer and the judge entered the room, there were two sides to the courtroom: the victims' side and the murderer's side, divided by a central aisle. That is how we had seated ourselves, how we had divided ourselves.

Jesse's uncle had seen Gil's first contact with Jesse's mother, months ago, in this very room, when Gil had walked over to Debra Carr, offered condolences, and extended her hand. Today, the same uncle was seated just to my left, on the other side.

As usual, he was segregated from us, across the aisle, over with the murderer's family. I sat five feet from him. He was to my left. He seemed to have depths of kindness in his profile. As I watched, he turned to look back into my eyes. I nodded at him, and in response, he rose. Gently, he stood. A little stiffly, he crossed that immeasurable aisle. He put out his hand. And then, the miracles began.

Morgan's papa Dan was to my right. Jesse's uncle held his hand out to Dan. This would be first contact between Jesse's family and Morgan's papa, who would, in a few minutes, be asked to take the witness stand and deliver his impact statement to the judge. Dan took his hand.

Jesse's uncle apologized first to Dan, then to Gil. Leaning close and doing the best he could in a very few seconds--though distraught--Mr. Carr was evangelical and sincere. Before he went back to his seat, nine other people in his family slowly rose.

They were all on that other side of the aisle, where they had expected to sit, loathed and untouchable. They were all rising to come across that aisle. One by one, men and women, Jesse's relatives, waited their turn, and they all offered their hands to Dan, and reached over to Gil. They all apologized, and many wept.

Dan and Gil accepted them all.

I felt the courtroom somehow converging with different energy, a dimension which most of us hear about in Sunday school. This procession across the aisle was a sacred, spontaneous enactment of the oldest and deepest wisdom, to do the least damage and the most good, to choose healing over hatred, and mercy over power.

Jesse's mother rose last. Like Lazarus, she followed some external imperative. Unsteady, she walked uneasily toward the aisle. Unlike her family members, she could go no further. She could not step or reach into the territory of the victims.

She stood alone, unable to proceed beyond the small space she occupied in the aisle, without a plan, the most castigated woman in the Commonwealth. She simply stood.

This was the place where she had to stand, awaiting her own sentencing.

I saw Gil rise. She approached Jesse's mother. In that aisle, in the great divide of humanity, where difficult choices are made, to battle evil, to author theories of exclusion and superiority, to offer kindness, to crusade, Gil stepped and raised both arms. She gently, silently enfolded Jesse's mama. Two mamas, now in one cocoon, leaning on each other's shoulders, intimate, exhausted, but determined. Determined, together.

Forgiveness is not what I saw. In their embrace, I saw raw, unexpected, unguarded, unjudgmental compassion.

They whispered back and forth to one another. Later, Gil told me what she and Jesse's mother had said to each other, as they hugged in that usually irredeemable and infertile space between families.

Will you always pray for me, Gil? Yes, I will pray for you, Debra.

Will you pray for me, Debra? I will always pray for you, Gil.

The richest blessings take work and skill to recognize, accept, and foster. Miracles require that we shed all clinging vestiges of hate. If we can manage our part in a miracle, then, tentative at first, like a hyacinth blossom unfurls, joy will open again. When it finally opens, like a hyacinth, joy will open in all directions.

And the air is sweet again.

Jane Lillian Vance,
Morgan's teacher in the last Spring of her life

—⁓—

A final poem for you, my Morgan.

241,
Always,
Mama

Finally,
Morgan, promise fulfilled

We caught the guy who killed

Mogo
Now you can go

Yes dear
Loose the bonds that tether you here

Let your soul soar like it should
Morgan Harrington dead for good

Fly, Dragon-dancer, baby girl
Into the next world.

Listen, now: it's Morgan's song:

Dear God

I wanna grow
Like cicadas grow

Getting so big, robust and stronger
That my skin can't hold me any longer

And I'll split at the seam of my back and climb out

Out of my shell--swell--
Though naked and frail, I won't fail

Chrysalis
I want this

Not forced to change by sadness and decay, no way

I want to burst forth into transformation
In full joyous throbbing song

Just like God made-a
The cicada

That's the way

And I choose--

Launch

To learn about supporting Help Save the Next Girl, please visit
helpsavethenextgirl.com.

To support the efforts of the Morgan Harrington Educational Wing at
Orphan Medical Network International's OMNI Village in Ndola, Zambia,
please go to *omnimissions.com.*

To support the Morgan Dana Harrington Memorial Scholarship at the
Virginia Tech Carilion School of Medicine, please visit
give.to.vt@vt.edu, or call 540-526-2205.

To view Jane Lillian Vance's art, please visit
janevance.com.